UNLOCK COLLECTIVE GENIUS
How to make space for creativity and co-creation

BISPUBLISHERS

Unlock Collective Genius

How to make space for creativity and co-creation

Alwin Put

For Annelies, Magnus and Svante
Our space is sacred to me.

Visit our website www.captainsofleadership.com for more information about our events, training and facilitation services.

Copyright © 2024 Alwin Put and BIS Publishers

BIS Publishers
Timorplein 46
1094 CC Amsterdam
The Netherlands
+31 (0)20 515 02 30
bis@bispublishers.com
www.bispublishers.com
www.captainsofleadership.com

ISBN 978 90 636 9723 5

Cover and inside design, illustrations: Tine van Wel, tinevanwel.nl
Final editing: Julie Harris

All rights reserved. No part of this publication may be reproduced or transmitted in any form or by any means, electronic or mechanical, including photocopy, recording or any information storage and retrieval system, without permission in writing from the copyright owners. Every reasonable attempt has been made to identify owners of copyright. Any errors or omissions brought to the publisher's attention will be corrected in subsequent editions.

Contents

Introduction — 13

Part 1: The Concept of Making Space — 17

CHAPTER 1: The Dimensions of Space — 19
CHAPTER 2: From Collaboration to Co-creation — 35

Part 2: The 5 Tenets of Making Space — 51

CHAPTER 3: The Switch — 53
CHAPTER 4: The Hook — 81
CHAPTER 5: Depatterning — 113
CHAPTER 6: Anchoring — 155
CHAPTER 7: Inception — 177

Part 3: Unlock Collective Genius — 201

CHAPTER 8: Make Space for Meetings and Workshops — 203
CHAPTER 9: Make Space for Life — 213

Afterword — 221

Glossary — 224
Acknowledgments — 227

Are you a Vaganaut?

Vaga – naut
A person who enjoys making space to explore the potential of collective genius in synergy with others, investing their full attention in a shared moment.

Vaga– (derived from "vagal"): relating to, mediated by, or being the vagus nerve.
–naut: indicating a person engaged in the navigation of a vehicle, esp. one used for scientific investigation.

FOREWORD
By Julie Harris, editor and co-creator of Unlock Collective Genius

IN THE EARLY years of my career, working with science committees, tax committees, and privacy committees at Paris' Organisation for Economic Co-operation and Development (OECD) from 1995–2005, I sat through countless meetings that seemed to go, well, I don't know where. Intelligent, accomplished people from all around the world would gather around a large conference table, seated behind their country flags, ostensibly to solve pressing global challenges. And yet, more often than not, we'd go in circles, rehashing familiar arguments, unable to access the collective wisdom in the room.

Participants were physically present but not truly engaged. They'd come with prepared statements and speeches, from which they seemed to rarely depart. Two-day committee meetings were dominated by these pre-crafted scripts, leaving little room for fresh content or the spark of true action. Everyone seemed to go along with the program, replaying old, well-worn patterns. Something was missing, some secret ingredient we hadn't yet discovered to transform those stagnant sessions into fountains of insight and innovation, action and impact.

Fast forward to 2022, when I had the opportunity to facilitate a session at the OECD on external communications with the Governing Board of the Centre for Educational Research. This time, something was different. From the first moments, you could feel a shift – a sharpening of attention, an opening of minds among the delegates, online and off. People truly listened to each other, building on ideas rather than defending positions, exploring uncharted territory together with curiosity and enthusiasm. In that crucible of authentic co-creation, solutions emerged that none of us could have conceived on our own. I left energized and inspired, determined to decode the alchemy that allows a group to access its collective genius.

This is why I believe Alwin Put's new book, *Unlock Collective Genius*, is so vitally important for our times. Having been a fan of Alwin's work since his groundbreaking *Captains of Leadership*, I knew I was in for a breakthrough with this new book. And it did not disappoint. Blending relatable stories, philosophical musings, and immediately applicable practices, *Unlock Collective Genius* offers both a mindset and a skillset for "making space" – fostering the conditions that allow people to connect deeply, think expansively, and co-create fearlessly.

The 5 tenets Alwin outlines – the Switch, the Hook, Depatterning, Anchoring, and Inception – are deceptively simple yet transformative when practiced with devotion and nuance. My favorite chapter on Depatterning reveals how our entrenched habits of thought and behavior keep us stuck in superficial interactions, and offers tools to disrupt those patterns and access novel ways of relating and creating. As Alwin aptly writes, "You can't read the label when you're stuck inside the bottle." This chapter validates the intuitive sense in all of us that there is immense value in forgiving ourselves for where we are, breaking out of groupthink, and doing what we need to do to "let our genius out."

Whether you are a facilitator by profession or simply someone committed to having more meaningful and generative conversations, there will be insights and invitations here for you. I encourage you to engage with this book not as a passive reader but as an active experimenter. Try on the ideas and practices, discuss them with colleagues and friends, make them your own. Some of what Alwin shares may feel obvious, some of it counterintuitive. Release any judgment and stay curious. Whenever you feel your attention slipping in a meeting, or a planning session, getting stuck, reach for one of Alwin's tenets and see what shifts.

My greatest hope is that *Unlock Collective Genius* sparks a revolution of conscious co-creation. That in teams and organizations around the world, people begin showing up more fully, listening more bravely, and connecting more deeply, liberating the untapped creativity and wisdom waiting in the spaces between us. Imagine the impact this could have – more innovative solutions to complex challenges, more engaged and fulfilled employees, more organizations thriving in times of change. As Alwin so eloquently shows, this is not just a nice-to-have in our age of complexity; it is an imperative for solving the thorny problems we face, and creating a world that works for all.

May this book be your catalyst and companion on that journey.

Julie Harris

INTRODUCTION
Above the clouds

The plane was nearly full, with just a few vacant seats remaining. A friendly steward flashed a warm smile as he helped some passengers find space for their carry-ons. Beside me, a middle-aged woman unpacked her knitting supplies, preparing to keep herself occupied during the two-hour flight from Rome to Brussels. Soft sunlight filtered through the clouds outside my window. I gazed out, my thoughts drifting back to the workshop I had just spent the last two days facilitating, until the pilot's warm voice announced our take-off.

It was Thursday morning, and I had dedicated most of that week to guiding a large group of professionals through developing a strategic plan.

Getting to know new people while collaborating toward a shared goal has always been the highlight of my work. A deep connection emerges naturally when everyone is intensely focused on a common objective. Of course, there's an initial awkwardness, as no one quite knows what to expect – whether they're headed for comfort or discomfort. But once the group finds its groove, the different personalities start making their voices heard. The hard work and passionate discussions yield satisfying results, leaving participants with a significant sense of purpose and belonging to this newly formed collective.

Diversity within a group is invaluable, injecting a rich array of perspectives into every conversation. Stories and anecdotes, thick with emotion, fill the room as people open up to different viewpoints on the topics at hand. You can see the various roles take on distinctive personas: the *rational thinkers* constructing frameworks, the *governors* fixated on KPIs and policy, seeing their world as an ordered environment where rules will be followed, the passionate *realists* trying to convince everyone of their gritty "ground truth," the creative *problem-solvers* getting caught up in generating "the solution" while leaving little room for dissent.

All these different personalities, each symbolic of their roles and steeped in the organizational culture, are brought together in one space. I ignite the interactions as a facilitator while their voices and opinions fuel each other. It's a dynamic I never tire of witnessing.

This most recent workshop displayed familiar patterns in the group dynamics like so many before it. Conversations tended to go in circles. Most contributions drew from personal perspectives rather than what participants had learned from clients. People got so absorbed in the conversational weeds that they struggled to extract the core insights. Several ducked out or checked their messages mid-discussion. Some were perpetually late returning from breaks. The intrinsic motivation and sense of ownership weren't consistently high.

Yet despite these patterns, this workshop yielded a positive outcome and aligned the key stakeholders. All the participants expressed gratitude and recognized the value of having the workshop. Still, I couldn't quite share their level of satisfaction. Did we get everything out of that shared moment? Seeing satisfied participants is gratifying, but I can't say I was equally satisfied. Was I being too self-critical about my facilitation and the group's engagement? Or was there something more I should have explored?

As our plane lifted off from Fiumicino Airport, my neighbor immediately began knitting what would likely be a cozy new scarf for someone – probably a calming ritual to ease any flying jitters. I turned my gaze back toward the rapidly shrinking Rome below. Before the workshop, I had spent a fun weekend there sightseeing with my wife and sons. While extremely crowded with tourists at every attraction, it was still a blast. Having visited Rome before, its beauty was expected rather than surprising to me this time – kind of like the workshop, enjoyable but familiar.

As we ascended, my view shifted from the densely packed cityscape toward the suddenly visible Mediterranean. The vastness of that open sea eclipsing the manmade structures and congested human activity was jarring. That vivid contrast immediately struck me – the packed city's cramped stuffiness versus the waters' liberating expanse. At that moment, I grasped a feeling I had been unable to articulate until now, overwhelmed by the visceral sensation of such unobstructed openness sprawling out before me.

In a trance-like state, I watched little boats leaving wandering trails across that vast emerald-green surface, fully immersing myself in the boundless visual. And then, just as quickly – poof! Our plane entered the clouds. The scene dissolved into a formless white and gray haze. It dawned on me that these clouds were a perfect metaphor for how our thinking can become muddied and obscured when we collaborate in workshops: stuck in repetitive patterns, blind to the bigger picture and unexplored possibilities beyond our fixated line of sight, lacking a vision of anything except what lies immediately in front of us. Yet just as abruptly, that fog parted again – poof! I was graced again with an expansive outlook, seeing clearly for miles. It was the same feeling as having an epiphany.

And that's when it crystallized for me.

I need to explore how we can spend more time "above the clouds" in meetings and workshops when people are co-creating solutions. When they are seeking change and new futures. We must make space for true novelty to emerge, rather than remaining constrained within our usual insular confines, within our "clouds." All the workshops I've facilitated contained some notion of open "space" for exploration, but more often than not, that space wasn't deep or expansive enough to unleash real innovation, to "unlock collective genius."

This is what sparked me to write this book about making space to co-create.

PART 1
The Concept of Making Space

Dear Diary,

Well, this is a first. The first time I am writing you. Lately, I've been experiencing feelings of overwhelm quite a bit, maybe even some anxiety. There's always so much going on. There are so many things I have to take care of, but there's also so much stuff that steals my attention. I have a hard time just relaxing in the moment. My mind goes all over the place when I am not busy doing a specific task. I even have a hard time giving someone I care about my full attention when I am with them. I sometimes wish I had more space for something, for someone. I wish the world would stop for a minute – just a minute … What a strange concept this is, "space." How can I not grasp what "space" really is and, at the same time, crave it? Is it time? A pause? A break from everything? Silence …? I wish I understood it better so I could figure out how to get more of it.

Your Vaganaut

CHAPTER 1.
THE DIMENSIONS OF SPACE

WHAT IS SPACE? It is not merely physical. So what is it? It seems abstract, yet we often use the expression "making space" for something. It feels like there is a *scarcity* of space. We wish we had more space sometimes. We have to make space to allow for something to happen. Space isn't just there by default. What is this space? What does it consist of?

There are many different ways of looking at "making space."

Let's look at a couple of real-life stories to illustrate the space we will explore.

BOARDGAMES DURING LUNCH

I was driving my son to soccer practice. After a day at school, he is usually less talkative, but today, there was something on his mind that he wanted to share with me.

He said, "Dad, I understand now why you are giving us a hard time about obsessively playing games on our mobile phones or watching TikTok."

That caught my attention immediately. Whenever my sons have nothing to keep them busy at home, they reach for their phones and morph into a zombie-like state, playing games or watching TikTok. When they spend too much time on their screens, their brains seem to switch into half-awake mode. Normal human interaction becomes a challenge. But now my oldest one is reflecting on this behavior. This is interesting, to say the least.

I respond, keeping my enthusiasm in check, "Tell me more. What opened your eyes?"

He explains that during every lunch break at school, his friends turn into the zombies I always talk about. Glued to the screens of their mobiles as if the real world doesn't exist. He usually joins them for a while, but today he suddenly realized how sad it is to waste that time together by being caught up in your own world. I might have had a little influence with my preaching the day before about how we used to have so much fun in school, experiencing true camaraderie, playing tricks on each other and the teachers, and talking about the songs and movies we love during our breaks.

He continued explaining how he told one of his friends, "Shouldn't we be having more fun playing games together in real life instead of virtually? It seems odd that we are playing a game online together, but we're all separate on our screens." His friend liked the idea, and they suggested to the others that they quit playing on their phones and join them in having some real-life fun. They didn't feel like it, and the idea was dropped. Everyone continued playing the virtual game.

With a look of disappointment, he tells me, "I get so jealous when you talk about your childhood, playing with your friends in the streets during holidays and having so much fun clowning around during breaks at school. I wish I could have that kind of fun with my friends."

I knew there and then it was the golden opportunity to win the battle of "screen time." I had him right where I wanted and immediately devised an idea to help him get his friends off their devices and into real-life friendship. I told him right there in the car, "Why don't you bring that 18+ board game to school tomorrow with the explicit statements about shit that happens in life? I'm sure that will get their attention." My son is nearly 13 years old, and the game didn't have offensive or sexual content; it seemed fine. It was also the best thing I could think of at that moment to help him win over the attention of his friends.

The next day, he came home and immediately approached me with a big smile. He said, "They loved it. They all put down their phones, and we played the game for as long as the lunch break lasted. They said they wanted to play it again tomorrow. It was so much fun, Dad; we laughed out loud and told each other stories we never told before. Things we have experienced. Stories triggered by the game cards. I might bring some different games to school in the coming days. I feel I am having fun with my friends like you had when you tell me about your childhood."

When they played their collaborative games online, like Brawl Stars, they connected as well. Still, it wasn't the same level of connection. There was no space created for stories, for listening, for bonding.

My boy and his friends decided to make some space for a game together. This allowed them to connect more deeply.

A few weeks later, I asked my son how things were going during his lunch breaks. He told me they still played games and chatted now and then, but some of his friends couldn't leave their phones aside and tended to get sucked into the online games again, which eventually made his other friends do the same. He predicted that the board games would have the staying power of a bubble in a windstorm.

Making space for something is about deliberately ruling out distractions so something or someone can receive our full attention.

SPACE TO BREATHE

As I began my run, the early morning world was just stirring to life. The rising sun cast a warm glow, burning off the wispy fog above the ponds. Though the trees stood bare, tiny buds hinted at the lush foliage to come. A serene quiet blanketed the area – in the past 10 minutes, I had passed only one other soul.

I focused on keeping my mind clear, tuning into the rhythm of my breathing. The crisp air felt invigorating yet still held winter's chill. I could feel it flowing smoothly in through my nose and out through my mouth, my cadence settling into a steady 3-count inhale, 3-count exhale pattern. Finding my stride often takes me a little while, but I'll ease into a 4-count rhythm once I do. Periodically, I hummed slightly on the exhales. I had read that this subtle humming helps dilate your blood vessels for better flow. More than that, I enjoyed how it relaxed me and regulated my out-breath.

Up ahead, a muddy puddle blocked my path. I prepared to leap over it with a couple of wider strides. This brief burst caused my heart and respiratory rates to pick up momentarily. But once past the puddle, I quickly re-established my earlier rhythm. My inhales grew a bit deeper for a few cycles as I regulated, elongating the exhales to match until I was back to my usual steady cadence.

I aimed to fully embody the rhythm rather than just consciously maintaining it. Gazing out at the horizon, I cultivated a sense of oneness with my surroundings. This unitive feeling brought tranquility for a little while until my mind started drifting to an upcoming meeting I needed to be home for. I reassured myself it would all work out, then refocused my attention on my breathing.

Midway through my route, the path sloped up a small hill, demanding more effort and disrupting my stable breathing pattern. I charged with vigor as if conquering this incline was the day's most important task. Soon, I felt challenged to keep inhaling solely through my nostrils – that hungry sensation of needing more air was creeping in, stirring the urge to open my mouth and gulp in bigger breaths. But I resisted, continuing to breathe in through my nose while accepting the impulse for more air. "This makes me feel alive," I told myself, "Reminding me how vital this process is." My mind was trained to be hyper-attuned to maintaining a slow, steady respiration pattern precisely when that air hunger arose. I crested the top, relishing the triumph, then allowed myself to recover and re-establish a smooth rhythm on the descent.

My run was nearing its end as my house appeared ahead. It was time for the "power sprint" – my ritual of running with a tall, powerful stride while engaging my full body. As I picked up speed, I tightened every muscle with intensity yet allowed myself to breathe in through my mouth. This oxygen boost gave me a surge of energy, leaving me feeling invincible by the time I reached home. It was like a condensed power pose in perpetual motion.

Almost there now, I slowed to a walk for my final cooldown strides. This transition let me gradually regulate my breath back down to that 4-count rhythm. When I arrived at my doorstep, I felt grounded and centered, mind and body in harmony – ready to take on whatever the new day might bring.

Over the past five years, I had had a keen interest in breathwork. I first learned about the importance of it when learning how to meditate. For a while, I solely associated breathwork practices with that meditative context. Then I stumbled upon an article revealing the unhealthy breathing habits so prevalent in our fast-paced, modern society, especially the West. One thing led to another until I ultimately took my first formal breathwork course, devouring every popular book on the subject I could find. To be honest, I became a bit obsessive in my pursuit of breathwork knowledge. But after a while, keeping up with a routine of breathwork practices started feeling forced. There was an overload of information available. There was always some new technique to learn. And I suffered a severe case of FOMO. So, I decided to let go and only pay attention to my breathing patterns instead of forcing it with various techniques.

During my run, I simply aimed for the most balanced state by breathing as slowly and steadily as I could while engaging in the physical tension of exercising. To maintain that steady rhythm, I only needed to consciously downregulate my breath whenever it got disrupted – like dodging that puddle or climbing the hill, taking me out of my rhythm. Making breath awareness an automatic habit enabled me to self-regulate my nervous system efficiently. My running became a regular practice of building breath awareness and mild regulatory conscious breathing.

When I was voraciously consuming book after book and course after course on breathwork, I kept cramming more and more information into an increasingly narrow headspace. Much of what I was taking in ultimately proved extraneous; I was packing it all in without any room to fully process or embody the wisdom. Only once I let go of that analytic intensity, giving myself time to experiment and experience the principles

I had learned with unassuming self-observation, could I finally metabolize the knowledge into sustainable behavior. Now, breathwork has become integrated into my psyche – the awareness is ingrained, and the prescribed techniques happen naturally without much directed effort.

Breathwork wasn't the only capability I tried to build by stuffing my brain with knowledge. Whenever I felt I was behind on knowing about popular topics like growth hacking, Design Thinking, emotional intelligence, healthy eating, leadership, etc., I would look for all the important books and courses to study. In hindsight, the most useful and only insights that lasted were the ones I gained from experience. That is, experience coming from making space to consciously putting things into practice.

Making space to explore knowledge and gain insights to the point where it becomes wisdom is a fundamental part of any learning process.

LOOKING IN THE MIRROR

I have noticed the frowning a couple of times now. And it is hard to see any facial expressions in this online Microsoft Teams call. Each person comes from a different part of the world and has varying internet connection quality. Some sit very close to their camera, while others have a different and often peculiar position in front of the camera. One person is barely surfacing from the bottom of the screen as if she just climbed up a ladder to reach out and show her face through a small window. Another person looks down from above as if the chair he is sitting on is higher than the desk on which the laptop and camera are placed. Sensing the group's level of energy and enthusiasm is a challenge, especially because I am doing most of the talking in this kick-off call for the Captains of Leadership Facilitation Training.

In my previous book, *Captains of Leadership: Build your Facilitative Confidence*, I explain the simple core principles of great facilitation. The book is less about facilitation techniques and more about the soft skills necessary to blend a group of people into an amazing, synergetic moment. Since the book's launch, I have been helping people develop these soft skills in on- and offline courses. This time, the course happened online with a diverse group of people. Diversity is key to making this training experience compelling. Each participant delivers a mini-workshop during the course. The more diverse the participants are, the more diverse these mini-workshops become. The easier it is for me as a trainer to cover all the different angles of facilitation.

I didn't only notice the frowning; I felt it. It was distracting. It also caught me by surprise. In all the previous training sessions, participants had been curious and open to hearing about the journey they were about to embark on. This time, it clearly generated some confusion, particularly with this participant. After a couple of frowns, I paused my explanation of the training approach and checked in with her.

I asked, "Is everything clear so far, and do you feel comfortable with this approach?"

She replied, "I don't understand what you want us to do. What topic do you want us to prepare a workshop for? Shouldn't we receive a clear assignment for the workshop? How else can we learn in a structured way what an effective workshop looks like?"

I tried to reassure her that the learnings would eventually be structured according to a framework and that we would simulate the same "being thrown in the deep end" feeling facilitators often have to deal with. I noticed she wasn't completely satisfied with my answer. I made a mental note to ensure I provided enough structure for her to feel comfortable in the training.

A few weeks later, we had our first full training session, and two participants delivered their mini-workshops, facilitating them with the other participants as their workshop team. They were fabulous and, luckily, showed some typical facilitation hiccups that allowed me to explain some new insights to the group.

Before I explain anything after a mini-workshop, I first give the floor to the participants to share their views. The same participant brought her frowning and furrowed brow to this session as well. Her expression of confusion and critical thinking put me on high alert because I had to make sure everyone felt safe enough to show some vulnerability while sharing their reflections about the mini-workshop experience.

When it was her turn to share her thoughts, all my attention was on the group, ensuring I would immediately notice any sign of discomfort. Her explanation was extremely smart and eloquent. She almost took over the role of trainer. With each observation she shared, she also provided a very structured recommendation on how to improve it, often checking my reactions to detect my astonishment at her intelligent contributions.

What she said was great stuff; it was smart but lacked empathy and often insight into the motivation behind people's behavior. The recommendations felt methodical. They would make complete sense if the world and its humans were a logical and predictable place, void of emotions and erratic behavior. I wanted to keep her motivated, so I worked with it. She perceived my going along with it as an acknowledgment of her skills and capability, and the frowning was replaced with an open expression. The rest of the group was still enjoying every bit of it, and it didn't feel like they were intimidated by her way of giving feedback.

We made a lot of progress during the following sessions. The participants worked through several abstract concepts to arrive at great insights about human behavior and their facilitative power to lead. The contributions from the "frowning lady" became a bit softer as some of the insights brought up by the group surprised her and broadened her perspective. She became convinced that the training could actually have some new learnings for her, and it wasn't a waste of her precious time. I also noticed during the course of the training that I earned her trust. She remained overly structured and directive when providing her recommendations and sometimes a little bit pedantic when giving her feedback. Still, it was well-balanced with the style of other participants and thereby contributed to a nice level of diversity and variety.

In the last session, it was her turn to facilitate her mini-workshop. I had already had a separate call with her to provide some coaching during the preparation of her mini-workshop. With all other participants during their prep/coaching calls I was able to introduce some interesting new approaches for their workshop flow, which created some excitement. She was only interested in telling me what her workshop flow would be and explained all the smart little twists she added to it to arrive at the desired result with the group.

There was no room for me to question or add anything else. Her idea of the coaching call was for me to be astonished again by her capabilities and to confirm that she was already incredibly good at leading co-creative sessions. I could already see where her flow could become challenging to deliver; it had elements that were too directive and too structured, with little room for interpretation or creativity. There were too many breakout conversations in too little time and insufficient time for plenary consolidation. It surprised me that she integrated an interesting twist at the end, asking the participants to keep their conclusions in mind and imagine how they would express them as advice to their kids. I didn't expect her to craft such an empathy-driven ending into her workshop flow. I couldn't help but feel a little bit proud for having triggered this kind of thinking with the learnings from the training so far.

She started off a little nervous, which confirmed my hunch that she had a perfectionist personality that forced her to strive to bring her absolute best. The nervousness at the start changed into a gracious and elegant facilitation, which astonished me. It hinted at a schoolteacher style, reminding me of Julie Andrews in "The Sound of Music." At times, she couldn't help but become too directive when the group didn't come up with the answer she already had in mind. Her ending was clearly out of her comfort zone. She was hesitant when she gave the instructions to the participants to articulate the conclusions with the simplicity used when advising children. Because of the hesitance, the participants didn't get it at first, but then they finally tried to meet her expectations. The confusion about the instructions made her feel even less comfortable. She felt vulnerable after finishing her workshop and moving into the feedback/reflection part of the training.

Everyone was kind and gentle. I had to nudge them to explain more in depth how they experienced the facilitation. She was used to receiving praise for her leadership skills, especially when leading meetings and workshops. This time, the participants expressed how they didn't seem to have a lot of room to think for themselves and make their own conclusions. The instructions were clear but firm. Sometimes, the facilitator expressed conclusions that the group didn't make themselves. These were imposed on them. They were able to share thoughts but weren't able to have deeper conversations and deal with different opinions. The facilitator talked a lot, and no one dared to interrupt or question her. The ending was fun but felt out of place compared to the rest of the flow of activities. In general, they felt a lot of trust in her leadership but also a reluctance to speak out fully and explore the topic broadly. As gracious and elegant as she was in giving instructions, that same style was applied when taking in the feedback. I was in awe.

She explained to the group at the end of the training that she hadn't been sure this course would bring her anything. She was convinced about her facilitation and leadership skills. Throughout the course, however, she had started to feel more uncertain about herself as a facilitator. By the time she had to deliver her mini-workshop, she explained that she felt very nervous. When delivering her workshop, she regained her confidence and felt it went very well, precisely as she had planned. The feedback during the reflection round opened one blind spot after the other, she said. "I never imagined this is the effect my leadership style has. I was convinced I always provided the right answers for people to get to the best place in the most efficient way. Now I understand I didn't nurture co-creation and risked not taking everyone along with my directive approach. It is such an eye-opener that I leave little room for people to find their own answers and how I am not creating any intrinsic motivation to take action, depriving them of ownership."

These self-reflective breakthrough moments can only happen if you make the space to really see yourself through different eyes. A smart person once told me, "You can't read the label when you're stuck inside the jar." Thank you for that wisdom, Julie. That is exactly what happened here. Because there was enough space to make a subject-object shift, this participant could see herself from some perspectives that weren't visible previously. Without the necessary space, you act as the subject, seeing what you want to see, missing out on your blind spots that carry so much growth potential.

Making space is essential to see things from another perspective, empathize with others, step out of your identity, and objectively observe yourself.

SPOON CARVING FOR PRESENCE
I arrived at a stranger's house, utterly clueless about who lived there or what lay in store. Knowing my affinity for workshops, a good friend decided to combine our worlds by gifting me a rather unusual birthday experience.

This friend is an arborist by trade – a true tree lover and wood enthusiast. It's an interesting combination. When he has to cut down trees for legitimate reasons, he ensures the timber gets repurposed for various purposes by different craftspeople. Including, as it turned out, providing the raw materials for this particular workshop focused on carving, of all things, wooden spoons.

The invitation instructed me to pass through a gate next to the house and make my way toward the garden, where I'd find the "spoon-carving shed." Following the directions, I could already detect that distinctive campfire scent wafting through the air, evoking a sense of adventure. After navigating past some shrubbery, I was delightfully surprised to discover a cozy wooden shed with a couple of guys hacking away on a tree trunk, slowly unearthing the golden spoon shapes hidden within. Peering inside, I saw an array of tools lining the wall, a warm stove in the corner, and a few chairs scattered across the wood-chip-covered floor – some topped with plush sheepskin rugs – and steaming mugs of coffee on nearby wooden stools.

The rustic setting immediately awakened my yearning to start chopping some wood. You might assume this is some stereotypical male fantasy, but I later learned that women love escaping to this weekly spoon-carving social gathering just as much as men do. Like the act of "spooning" itself, carving spoons transcends gender divides.

My friend and the warm, hospitable workshop host welcomed me before promptly presenting me with an assortment of logs harvested from various tree species to choose from. Since each type of wood has unique characteristics in terms of grain patterns and carving density, my initial selection would significantly influence the creative sculpting process. After about an hour of joyful chopping and cutting, I ended up with an extremely rough spoon shape that followed the natural whorls and knots of my log's grain.

What followed required more finesse than I anticipated. The host offered me a pair of protective gloves, then handed me an exquisite leather drawstring pouch containing a full set of specialized carving knives. The pouch had the unmistakable feel of an artist's toolkit – precious instruments designed to channel creativity and sophistication. I felt deeply honored, yet also a tad intimidated by the glimmering razor-sharp blades.

I'll admit I had grown rather impatient and overzealous during that first rough chopping phase, whittling away large chunks with reckless abandon in my efforts to unearth the ideal spoon silhouette. While careful and focused initially, after an hour or so, I became increasingly careless, chopping off too much repeatedly. This forced me to reimagine the overall spoon shape over and over again – a total of five times! Luckily, I still had enough trunk length to eke out one final rough iteration. What started as an intended large spoon became a much humbler, modestly-sized piece.

Once that rough silhouette finally emerged from the battered log, I was ready to swap my ax for those surgeon-like precision knives to delicately refine every subtle curve and hollow with painstaking detail. Anyone who has carved spoons knows that balanced symmetry is paramount. If the bowl (the concave portion that cradles the food) is too heavy while the neck (the transition from bowl to handle) is too thin and delicate, the spoon will snap while stirring your stew. Different spoon types exist for various intended uses, with both form and function dictating the ideal shape and aesthetic design.

I began whittling away, and after about an hour, I could feel that same restless impatience starting to resurface – the very thing that caused me to hack off too much wood earlier. This was when it became clear: the true essence of spoon carving isn't merely creating the most visually stunning piece but consciously slowing down to fully inhabit the present moment. You can't simply force your way toward sculpting beauty; you must become one with the wood itself. Only by immersing yourself in the immediacy of the work can you perceive the inherent artistry waiting to be released from within. If you aren't able to dial into that meditative state, you won't just end up with an unbalanced, nonfunctional, or outright ugly spoon – you're liable to draw your own blood in the process. Patience has never been my strongest suit. Had I neglected to wear those protective gloves, I'm sure I'd be short a few fingers by now.

But as I settled deeper into the rhythm, I savored the experience more and more. The longer I leaned into inhabiting each mindful moment and taking the time to meticulously shave away one gossamer curl at a time, the more I melded with the creative flow. My motions grew increasingly fluid and precise as the unique spoon shape I was birthing became lucid. I realized the calm, centered state I had reached felt worlds apart from my earlier antsy, hurried mindset. Our host clearly sensed the shift as well, complimenting my newly found carving prowess and the beautiful, balanced spoon steadily taking form.

By the end of the day, I felt genuinely amazed by the profound transformation that occurred from start to finish. I never anticipated how challenging it would be to simply slow down and reside in that moment – something I consciously strive to cultivate in every workshop and training session I lead. Yet here I was, struggling mightily with my impatience and resistance. From the moment I surrendered to the process, able to funnel all my focus into each achingly precise cut (likely aided by those razor-sharp knives heightening my senses), my envisioning abilities kicked into high gear. I could vividly perceive the future spoon's perfect form as it was being birthed into reality.

Accessing that level of creative flow requires space. Early on, I unconsciously resisted making that time and effort – I refused to create the space required for inspiration to take root. My mind kept getting preoccupied and distracted as I haphazardly made mistake after mistake, thoughtlessly following instructed tasks rather than truly creating anything authentic.

For any new vision, idea, or creative expression to emerge, you must first cultivate a sense of focused presence in the moment – you have to make space for creation.

YOUR MOST INVALUABLE RESOURCE

All the stories thus far have added a puzzle to the understanding of making space – an abstract concept that these narratives help to illustrate. Deeply connecting with others, accessing new levels of understanding about a subject, perceiving reality from an enlightening new perspective, and becoming utterly immersed in a creative endeavor – all these experiences rendering new insights, creativity, and growth have one thing in common that cultivate the required depth of space. Each story touches on the profound implications of our present-moment attentiveness.

These stories illustrate how making space is a result of how you invest your attention into the moment. Your attention is your most invaluable resource. In his book 'Indistractable', author Nir Eyal states that the ability to become indistractable is the skill of the century. He explains how mastering attention and focus enables individuals to achieve their goals, maintain productivity, and lead more fulfilling lives despite the myriad of distractions in the modern world. Your attention is limited, and at the same time, it is your superpower. Your attention has the capacity to amplify elements of your experience. The level of attention you can bring determines the level of amplification or the "depth of the space." With your attention, you can amplify the connection with other people, amplify learning, amplify perspectives, amplify creativity, …, anything you want to get out of that moment. Making space is, in essence, deliberately investing your attention.

Your attention has the capacity to amplify elements of your experience.

This principle of making space applies equally to our individual endeavors and any collaborative co-creation we engage in collectively. You can make space for a personal moment, and you can make space for a shared moment. Making space for a shared moment and combining your attention with other people's attention can create resonance and enormous co-creative potential.

My objective in writing this book is to provide the language to communicate about the depth of space for co-creation and help people manage their attention more consciously together for better co-creative outcomes. By developing a more nuanced vocabulary for conveying space and its varying depths, along with practices for actively deepening space, a co-creative culture can be fostered that genuinely harnesses the catalyzing power of tapping into the collective intelligence. Such a shift feels critically necessary in this era where people are constantly overstimulated, frenetically "busy," and persistently distracted by technological lures, keeping the collective intelligence a mere latent possibility.

The practices of making space and managing your attention, as explained in this book, have the sole purpose of helping you generate better results from spending time together in meeting rooms and ensuring those better results are executed. I aim to impart wisdom, not just knowledge. Rather than bombarding you with statistics, frameworks, models, or elaborate graphs, I will render the abstract concept of space tangible with stories. This will help you relate more and enable you to communicate these ideas with your colleagues and develop your own tailored language and practices. While I may reference the scientific principles underlying certain concepts, my focus will not be on reiterating scientific findings. Instead, I will suggest approaches inspired by my experience observing and leading hundreds of workshops and meetings.

By delving into the practices presented in this book, I hope you'll consciously start experimenting with them to *make* space and *deepen* space when co-creating with others. This deliberate effort to make space will likely enhance your and your colleagues' awareness of its depth, fostering greater sensitivity to the level of attention present when sharing space. Developing practices, cultivating a shared language, and enhancing awareness will lay the foundation to build a culture for space.

As a reader of this book, you can become the instigator of a movement in your organization. With a critical mass of these space makers, meetings and workshops can transform from sources of dread to wellsprings of joy. Such environments promote stronger connections and satisfaction with outcomes, making shared moments feel like catalysts for project acceleration rather than time sinks.

The term "Vaganaut" is introduced intentionally to encourage space exploration beyond the confines of prescribed practices. My suggestions in this book are starting points, not limitations, designed to inspire further innovation in creating space. It is up to you whether my suggestions evolve into your own ways of making space. Are you a Vaganaut?

Let's explore!

Dear Diary,

I have started paying more attention to the things I care about in life. Whenever I enjoy doing something or being in the presence of other people, I try to experience every minute of it and not let my mind wander off so much. I even made a promise to myself that I would only check my phone a couple of times a day. I used to have it within reach all the time. It still feels strange, as if I am always missing something. I'm sure after a while I won't miss it at all. I got a compliment today at work. Someone said I am a good listener and so easy to talk to. I think I am starting to like this new habit of making more space. The conversation I had with my colleague was so much more interesting to me than before. For some reason, my being more present and showing more interest brought up a lot more interesting content. Or I just noticed a lot more things I could relate to. I wonder what effect it would have if everyone started making more space for good conversation at work? Maybe we would understand each other better and be more proactive about helping each other? I wonder if we would inspire each other more, like I was inspired today. Me, the "good listener," – who knew? What a great compliment to get.

Your Vaganaut

CHAPTER 2.
FROM COLLABORATION TO CO-CREATION

THEY HAVE BEEN holding their markers and sticky notes for a while now, but no one is writing anything down. Despite my prompts to capture their thoughts and stick them on the poster on the wall, nothing happens. All of them are completely absorbed in conversation, discussing all kinds of random solutions to the issues they seem to be confronted with daily. The conversation is deviating far from what I gave instructions for doing. One of the participants realizes I am observing the conversation and, with a puzzled expression, asks me again, "So, I'm sorry, but what are we supposed to do?"

A couple of weeks ago, I introduced this team to Design Thinking. They are tasked with radically improving their organization's services and were individually selected and invited to become part of this innovation team, on top of their day jobs. Having trained teams in Design Thinking before, I am always excited to observe another team finding its way with this approach, dealing with their organizational culture of innovation and the (usually) unrealistic goal setting from management. This time, however, it seems different. The organization appears to have a dynamic that allows for much flexibility and experimentation.

During the training part of this innovation track, I explained what I consider the two essential characteristics of Design Thinking. The first is the separation between the problem area and the solution area, meaning that the problem needs to be explored from different perspectives before any problem-solving can happen. If the two areas get mixed up, people explore the problem while already having a solution in mind, leading to a lot of bias and blind spots – innovation as usual for many organizations.

The other essential characteristic is the alternation between divergent and convergent thinking. This is probably the key to success for any approach in creative work. It means there is a conscious decision to spend time exploring beyond what you know, for example, by doing research or brainstorming. There is a conscious decision to end the broadening and move into connecting the dots and concluding all that has been generated or discovered. Being disciplined about separating the problem area from the solution area and alternating between divergent and convergent thinking speeds up the innovation process and makes the outcomes more qualitative.

Putting this newly acquired knowledge into practice created the expected challenges for the team. This was the first time they applied this thinking to innovate their services. I would have been surprised if they didn't jump into solutions while processing the client research they'd done. To be plucked out of your regular day-to-day activity and transform into a Design Thinking Innovation Wizard Wanda is a feat, even for the most experienced innovators. But despite all my nudging, they couldn't seem to stick to the problem area for now and kept discussing future solutions already. Whenever any observation about client challenges was mentioned, they didn't interpret and capture it; instead, I heard them throwing random solutions at each other. Divergent thinking instead of converging to outline what they knew about their clients so far.

Upon closer observation, I realized their discussion and solutions focused more on enhancing internal departmental operations than improving service delivery. They were trapped in a narrow, personal viewpoint, unable to shift toward understanding the service experience from their clients' perspective. Side conversations were sprouting up, yet there were still no sticky notes.

While the group was technically collaborating – allocating time to work together – the essence of their interaction fell short of true co-creation. At this stage in their creative process, they were expected to pool their findings about the current situation and collaboratively interpret these insights. Collectively empathizing with their clients. Generating a new depth of understanding of their clients' struggles and needs. This moment was meant to be a convergent step, identifying what else needs to be investigated before deciding what needs to be solved first. However, as participants continually circled back to their individual perspectives, the group strayed from recognizing research gaps. They lacked the space for interpreting new information and forming a new unified understanding of the client's perspective. The willingness to listen openly and welcome new insights was minimal, hindered by uncertainty about their roles and the superficiality of their contributions, which impeded deeper conversations. There surely was a form of collaboration happening, but no space for co-creation.

Despite groups like these embarking on endeavors to enhance their brands, products, or services with the best intentions and a solid grasp of methodologies, even in the presence of a facilitator, they often struggle to achieve the level of engagement necessary for breakthrough collective insights. They collaborate yet fail to cross the threshold into co-creation, merely echoing known information without generating the synergy needed for innovation.

Design Thinking and similar innovation methodologies quickly expose a group's capacity to make collaborative space. Creative sessions need space. Reflect on how many meetings you've attended today that had no real impact and could have been omitted without changing outcomes. You collaborated, but was there any form of co-creation? The value of shared moments increases with the depth of space created for them. If we meet each other and we don't have a good level of attention for that moment and each other, we are collaborating but not co-creating; it won't have a lot of impact. Conversely, intentionally creating space for these interactions can leave a lasting impression through new inspiration, crucial insights, a fresh perspective on work, and a sense of belonging that revitalizes us. That's when such a conscious effort to make space for the moment elevates the level of mere collaboration to become the co-creation of new and better outcomes for all involved.

Making space for co-creation is essential for an organization to unlock new potential and evolve.

When I prompted the group to indicate through a show of hands their confidence in empathically understanding client experiences through clients' eyes, they recognized a significant oversight. This realization spurred them into co-creating a strategy to conduct more client interviews, aiming to uncover and address their blind spots. The circular conversational ping-pong, blinded by single-minded personal perspectives, made way for purposefully and collectively strategizing for new client research. Their collective intelligence was ignited.

IS DESIGN THINKING DEAD?

Design Thinking, one of the more popular innovation methodologies in the last decades, has been criticized repeatedly by expert practitioners. Their critique makes a wonderful case to show the importance of making space to elevate collaboration to the level of co-creation. Co-creation being the act of conceiving something new into this world together, however big or small.

Making space for co-creation is essential for an organization to unlock new potential and evolve.

Design Thinking, a problem-solving methodology, traces its origins to Herbert Simon's seminal work, *The Science of the Artificial*, published in 1969. Although Simon did not explicitly name Design Thinking, his emphasis on human cognition and decision-making laid the foundation for its evolution. In the 1980s, organizations like IDEO, founded by David Kelly, Bill Moggridge, Mike Nuttall, and others, championed human-centered design. IDEO is renowned for creating iconic products and services, such as the first Apple mouse and the Swiffer mop. Alongside Stanford University's d.school, also established by David Kelley, and influential publications like "Design Thinking" in the *Harvard Business Review* in the early 2000s, IDEO propelled Design Thinking into mainstream awareness.

The Darden School of Business integrated it into its MBA curriculum in 2011, marking a significant academic milestone. Stanford's d.school further solidified its prominence by hosting the first Design Thinking conference, drawing global practitioners. By 2018, The World Economic Forum recognized Design Thinking as one of the top ten skills needed for the Fourth Industrial Revolution, a status further elevated during the COVID-19 pandemic due to its emphasis on empathetic collaboration and adaptability in virtual environments.

Today, Design Thinking is embraced worldwide across various sectors, with leading firms like IBM, Apple, Google, and Procter & Gamble at the forefront. Governments and the public sector are also leveraging it to improve policymaking and citizen services. The methodology's versatility and impact are evidenced by a wealth of articles, books, case studies, and academic courses.

Drawing from years of teaching Design Thinking across diverse industries, I've observed that its success hinges on participants' engagement levels throughout the process. True innovation challenges teams to stay aligned while interpreting information through empathy, maintaining connection throughout – from initial exploration to implementation. Therefore, applying Design Thinking is a perfect experiment to see whether organizations can make the necessary space to rethink their products and services from a human-centered perspective.

However, Design Thinking has faced scrutiny, highlighted by critiques like design professor Bruce Nussbaum's 2016 *Fast Company* article, "The Case against Design Thinking," and subsequent discussions questioning its efficacy. In 2017, "Why Design Thinking Won't Save You" was published in the *Harvard Business Review* by Natasha Iskander and Beth Kolko. In 2018, a controversial Medium post launched by designer and entrepreneur Joe Toscane, titled "Design Thinking is Kind of Like Syphilis," claimed

> *Design Thinking is a perfect experiment to see whether organizations can make the necessary space to rethink their products and services from a human-centered perspective.*

Design Thinking was overhyped. In 2019, "Design Thinking is Dead. What's Next?" was published in *Forbes* by Christian Madsbjerg, calling for a shift toward more culturally informed approaches to design and innovation. The discussion continues today on social media channels between believers and non-believers. Critics argue its hype has often led to superficial application, failing to yield substantial outcomes.

In my experience, organizations initially adopt Design Thinking as a set of rigid steps rather than embracing it as a philosophy to nurture creativity and empathy. Success stories are those where Design Thinking transcends procedural application to become a core part of organizational culture, often clashing with the dominant analytical thinking paradigm.

The answer to "Is Design Thinking dead?" is irrelevant. But the discussion is very interesting. For some people, Design Thinking never existed because they didn't know about it – and they could do their work perfectly fine without it. Some people tried Design Thinking in organizational cultures that weren't ready to question and research so many things in such an elegant dance of diverging and converging, let alone have the flexibility to swiftly adopt new ways of doing things. Some people work at design-driven organizations with many creative thinkers who have an innate ability to conceptualize from the abstract. They might feel Design Thinking has always been the way to go even before David Kelley and Tim Brown widely spread the idea of Design Thinking. In particular, people who make a living from Design Thinking are vocal about its being alive and not dead. The question is fueled with frustration about Design Thinking projects that have had disappointing results.

The right question to ask ourselves is: "Can we create enough space for co-creation in our organization full of distracted minds?" Observing such a wide conversation about the value of Design Thinking leads me to guess that many organizations can only honestly answer, "No, we can't. We face constant busyness, short attention spans, and decades of digital interruptions. There is no space to productively diverge and converge our way into radically smart evolutions and revolutions of our business."

The lack of deep space is the only reason co-creative methods like Design Thinking are called into question. It is the only reason people dislike their meeting culture. It is the only reason they are often out of tune with their intuition, unable to invent from the unknown, repeating only the known.

A MOMENT THAT MATTERS

A MOMENT IS NEVER JUST A MOMENT.
A MOMENT CAN BE MEANINGFUL.
A MOMENT CAN BECOME A BREAKTHROUGH.
A MOMENT CAN BE DEFINING.
AN EXPERIENCE THAT STANDS OUT.
MOMENTS CAPTURE A SPACE IN TIME
AND CAN MATTER TO THE PEOPLE INVOLVED.
A MOMENT CAN BECOME A LIFELONG MEMORY.
A MOMENT CAN BE THE START OF A NEW FUTURE.
OUR LIFE IS A TREASURE CHEST OF KEY MOMENTS.
OUR DECISIONS, WORLDVIEW, RELATIONS, BELIEFS AND VALUES
ARE SHAPED BY THE IMPACTFUL MOMENTS WE WERE PART OF.
MOMENTS THAT MATTER DON'T HAVE TO HAPPEN ONLY BY CHANCE.
MOMENTS CAN BE SHAPED WITH THE WISDOM OF TRUE LEADERSHIP.

This is what I believe in. Shaping a moment using the wisdom of true leadership is what I called "captaineering" in my previous book, *Captains of Leadership*. It is inspired by many great thinkers. Eckhart Tolle wrote about it in his famous work, *The Power of Now*; Mihaly Csikszentmihalyi wrote about it in *Flow*; Chip Heath and Dan Heath wrote about it in *The Power of Moments*; Priya Parker wrote about it in *The Art of Gathering*, and so many more.

Talking about the power of a moment feels like announcing the sky is blue. Yet, being in the moment and taking the time to connect seems to have become the hardest possible thing a modern human in the West can do. *The Power of Now* talks about our running minds crowding the space of the moment. *Flow* explains how distractions dismantle our best, focused, creative state. The *Art of Gathering* emphasizes the importance of having a shared clear purpose and fostering deep connections among those involved in a moment. *The Power of Moments* elaborates on requirements like "pride" and "elevation" to turn a moment into a lasting memory.

Looking back on all the workshops I have led in organizations, a few patterns emerge and seem to repeat themselves. Prejudices, concerns, and underlying friction fueled the running mind, clogging the creative channel. Overcrowded agendas, escalations, emails, and mobile messages kept minds busy, allowing little space for creation. A dulled sensitivity for meaning and purpose and bent, stretched, and sometimes broken, trust sucked the energy out of serendipity, preventing new breakthroughs.

How is it that we have perspective on the potential impact of moments, have even experienced life-changing ones, and may crave more of these powerful moments yet still fail to take ownership of the present by wasting away opportunities to create meaningful shared experiences? We understand the significance of living fully in the now but allow many chances to pass us by unseized rather than embracing them. We recognize the value of moments but don't actualize them. Why do we acknowledge the power of presence yet squander it, nevertheless?

ATTENTION SPAN

Gazing out the window at the Alps, I'm struck by the beauty of the landscape and filled with gratitude for my job as a facilitator. It's astonishing how fortunate I am to be here. The group, divided into three teams, is deeply engaged in the workshop activities. After three days of intense work, the room is adorned with posters and sticky notes. The view and the team's unwavering dedication are both gifts I cherish.

> *We recognize the value of moments but don't actualize them.*

The three-day flow I designed began with activities to collectively process our knowledge and spark inspiration for creating a new setup. The second day focused on gathering external inspiration and ideating, while the third day was dedicated to consolidating these ideas and setting a direction. It was an ambitious program, and I was uncertain if this group, whom I had never met before, could navigate it successfully.

At the workshop's outset, I gauged the group's energy, noting one individual with a cold and another adjusting from a different time zone. Yet, the overall vibe was promising, indicating potential for synergy. Day 3 should have given me a different feeling by now. I am used to people coming in late, leaving early, checking their messages and email during conversations, and stepping out randomly for an improvised coffee break without telling anyone as the workshop progresses. For some reason, people can forget the "work" part in workshop and mistakenly see it as a mere team-building activity. Those are always the first ones to start dipping in attention and engagement. Then, those who have a hard time letting go of their fixed mindsets get worn out from all the discussions their rigid thinking causes. They are the second group to start disengaging. What usually remains is a hardcore group who sees the workshop through until they feel they have achieved the objective. They stay engaged. Sometimes, this is a small group of Go-Getters Extraordinaire; sometimes, this group is still quite large.

This time it was everyone. I was stunned by the creativity and stamina of this group. They kept going straight to the finish, and when I observed them at the end, they looked like a proud sports team who had just won the game, feeling satisfied and ready for the next challenge.

Reflecting on this experience during my flight over the Alps, I was cooking up a storm in my brain kitchen trying to understand their secret: why had they been able to manage the depth of their space? How did they maintain such a level of attention to the present moment, which elevated their collaboration to qualitative co-creation? Suddenly, a light bulb went on.

Being in deep space is typical for a state of flow. A state when you are so deeply focused in the moment that you lose track of time, fully absorbed in what you are doing, performing your best without even trying too hard. It is a state of effortless concentration and enjoyment that can be experienced when playing sports or music or when intensely engaged in making art. This also happens in groups. When a group of people are working together smoothly and effectively. They feel like they are on the same wavelength, like a harmonious dance where everyone knows their part. While moving in sync, they create a sense of unity and mutual understanding. When a musician or band is "in the pocket," they are locked into the groove, with each member playing their part in sync with the others, resulting in a smooth and effortless feel to the music.

Practicing being in a flow state often can make it easier to enter that state more frequently. As with any skill you wish to develop, the more you practice entering a flow state, the more familiar you become with the conditions and activities that induce this state. Over time, you can learn to recognize the optimal conditions, such as having clear goals, receiving immediate feedback, being challenged at the right level, and being fully immersed in the task at hand. People who often engage in activities that require them to focus on the present moment and let go of distractions and self-doubt grow this second nature to get into flow. Jazz players experience this, just as people who do extreme sports like paragliding, off-piste skiing, and mountain climbing enhance their ability to engage fully with the task at hand every time they practice. Forest bathing and hiking can also hone your ability to enter flow states. By spending a lot of time in nature, you become more aware of your surroundings and engage more fully with the present moment. This heightened sense of awareness creates a mindset for entering flow states. An active lifestyle with plenty of physical activity is also known to help with entering flow states more easily.

Every member of this group practiced some kind of sport in nature. Most of them live close to the Alps; they go skiing or hiking every weekend, sometimes also on weekdays. Several of them own vans with beds installed, allowing them to escape into nature for as long as they want. Their main mutual interest areas were all about outdoor activities. Some were even dressed as if they were going on a hike while participating in the workshop. These people could easily fully engage in the present moment, deepening the space for co-creation for a full three days. They are flow seekers. Their attention span is trained by all those moments they spend in full focus or in nature's presence. It is very different from working with a group in which most participants get completely absorbed by this century's distractions and "carrots."

Although I am convinced the best thing any management of any organization could do to elevate as many moments as possible from mere collaboration to co-creation is to help their staff live an active life, spending a lot of time in nature and taking on hobbies that help them practice being in the moment, this book is not about promoting a particular lifestyle. I do not intend to convince you to adopt certain lifestyle practices and develop a specific mindset vis-a-vis life. I am, however, an enthusiast of "the shared moment."

The requirements for a flow state inspired me to develop the fundamental principles for making deep space.

The requirements for a flow state inspired me to develop the fundamental principles for making deep space to allow a co-creative moment to come to fruition. Clear goals, immediate feedback, challenging but not overwhelming tasks, focused attention, intrinsic motivation, and confidence to dive in and become one with a task and a team are factors that helped me develop powerful concepts that I will introduce in this book. These are concepts that I hope you will continue evolving as you share moments with others to co-create.

THE TENETS OF MAKING DEEP SPACE FOR CO-CREATION
Imagine standing at the edge of a cliff with your wingsuit on.

The wind whispers promises of adventure and freedom. With each gust, your wingsuit flutters like the wings of a bird preparing to take flight. Your heart dances with anticipation of the exhilarating plunge ahead.

Below, the view of a world stretched out in a breathtaking panorama of rugged mountains and lush valleys, painted in hues of green and gold by the setting sun. The distant horizon invites you to embrace the boundless skies and soar among the clouds.

In that moment, a rush of emotions floods your soul – excitement mingled with nervous anticipation, fear intertwined with a profound sense of awe. The adrenaline coursing through your veins is a potent elixir, fueling courage and igniting the fire of determination within …

Despite all the intimidating elements of nature you are facing, you are ready to jump. This calls for a firm "yes" to the adventure you are about to embark on. You are embracing this moment and consciously taking part in it. This is the first step of making space. The SWITCH.

As you gaze into the vast expanse before you, a feeling of deep connection to the untamed beauty of the natural world emerges, a sense of belonging that transcends words. With a final breath …

The lure for the adventure is strong. The reasons why you are attempting such a bold and challenging leap into the unknown are profound and lasting. You know what you are looking for when engaging in this activity. You know how this makes you feel. You are convinced of the value it can bring. This is the second step of making space. This step also deepens the space. It pulls your attention in. The HOOK.

You step into the void, surrendering to the embrace of gravity and the embrace of the wind. For a heartbeat suspended in time, you are weightless, a creature of the air, soaring on the wings of your dreams. In that fleeting moment of pure ecstasy, you know with absolute certainty that you are alive – truly alive – and that the world is yours to explore, one breathtaking leap at a time …

Letting go of control to fully explore the potential of bringing minds together in a shared moment. Soaring on the wings of your imagination and carried by the energy of the attention brought into this moment. The feeling of aliveness when new possibilities emerge. This is the third step, making space even deeper. The DEPATTERNING.

Yet amidst the chaos of the moment, a calm clarity settles over your soul like a gentle caress. With steady hands and unwavering focus, you adjust your body position, feeling the subtle shift of air currents beneath your wingsuit as you steer toward safety. In the distance, the landscape rushes toward you with dizzying speed, a blur of jagged cliffs and rolling hills that seem to blur into one. But you remained undaunted, your mind sharp and your instincts keen as you plot your course with precision and grace.

You are plotting your course while you are soaring through space. Adjusting the approach and navigating the unknown by marking what has become visible allows you to continue the journey with a sharp mind and keen instincts. This is the fourth step: maintaining a deep space for as long as necessary. The ANCHORING.

As the ground looms ever closer, you feel a surge of adrenaline course through your veins, a surge of determination that fuels your resolve. With a final burst of speed, you pull your parachute cord, feeling the fabric catch the wind with a triumphant whoosh.

And then, in a moment of sublime serenity, you are suspended in mid-air, drifting gently downwards like a feather on the breeze. The world around you slows down, and each breath is a sweet symphony of gratitude and relief.

As your feet touch the solid ground once more, you feel a surge of joy wash over you, a sense of triumph that echoes in the depths of your soul. For in that fleeting moment of perfect clarity, you had conquered not only the skies but also the doubts and fears that had once held you back.

With a smile upon your lips and a twinkle in your eye, you look out upon the horizon once more, knowing that the journey has only just begun. For you are a creature of the air, a dreamer of dreams, and the world is yours to explore, one breathtaking leap at a time.

The moment left a lasting mark. It planted a seed. The moment in space ends when all the insights have been packaged and strategized to become the start of change, of something new to be materialized. Although the co-creative moment that came to life is about to complete its purpose, more space is required to act upon the outcome. This is the fifth and final step, anticipating the depth of space necessary to take the next steps. The INCEPTION.

These 5 tenets for deep creative space will be explained in depth in the coming chapters within the context of co-creation. They tackle five common challenges people face to successfully bring about change in their organizations: weak intentions to be changemakers, lack of purpose to fuel the necessary grit to drive change, resistance to deep connection that allows for a level of synergy to create the change, the tendency to overcomplicate and overdesign conclusions and agreements, risking misalignment and scattered focus and, finally, a paralyzing skeptical mindset that deflates all motivation when confronted with organizational inertia and obstacles. All of the above are characteristics of lacking deep space. The tenets tackle these challenges by helping an involved group of collaborators make deep space for new realities to come to life.

In other words, these 5 tenets deepen space, ensuring sustained attention for improved outcomes, heightened motivation, and an increased capacity for action. They fuel a spirit of collectivity and catalyze collective movement. They "unlock collective genius."

In the upcoming chapters, you will gain a deeper understanding of each tenet and be introduced to practices that should help you achieve the goal of each tenet. Each practice will be broken down into parts you can reassemble in any way you like, building your own practices. It is hard to create a practice that works in every organizational culture across all industries. The idea is to inspire you with the philosophy behind each tenet and the techniques behind each practice so you can reinvent practices that fit your organizational culture.

With these 5 tenets, I would like to direct more attention to making space in our work lives as a counter-movement to all the stimuli we are bombarded with every minute of every day. These 5 tenets can help with finding group flow more easily when spending time together to co-create. The notion of making space will hopefully decrease our tendency toward busyness in our work lives, connecting us more with our intuition and each other. By creating a language for making deep space and providing purposeful practices, we are laying the foundation for evolved organizational cultures that allow for flow states in co-creation.

Dear Diary,

I am starting to perceive these moments I share with other people differently. All of them have some treasures, some gifts, to uncover. How odd that I never noticed this before. I was unexpectedly called into a meeting today, and right before I stepped in, I decided to try and make space again for it and give it my full attention. There was so much chatter and uncontrolled conversation that it was hard to follow at first. But when I gave it my full attention, without jumping in, I was able to observe some of the individuals' motivations behind their responses. I was able to read the room better and grasp people's overlapping stakes and concerns. When it was my turn to speak, I nailed it. I was spot on and so in tune with the moment and the people involved. People even thanked me for my input afterward, which felt a bit embarrassing. But I loved the state I was in. Inner calmness, almost serenity, but with my senses on high alert. Almost like a tiger, blended into the environment, no stress, but sharp as a razor's edge. I want more of this. I need to figure out the formula and perfect this ability to make space. I think I am on to something here. Can't wait to see what I figure out. Can't wait to see what I'll write you next time.

Your Vaganaut

PART 2
The 5 Tenets of Making Space

CHAPTER 3.
THE SWITCH

EVERYONE HAS RITUALS and routines to prepare for a given activity – to get in the right mood and mindset. Some are acted out deliberately. Others are more tendencies or habitual activities. Typically, people associate brushing their teeth with getting ready for bed. Getting dressed and putting on your make-up can be part of a morning routine, preparing yourself mentally to face the day's adventures.

Music bands have rituals to get in the mood to deliver a fantastic performance. Sports athletes have breathing techniques and visualizations to help them get in their zone. My personal ritual is visualizing long arms coming from my heart, hugging all the people who enter the workshop room, and thanking them for letting me facilitate their session. I know people who listen to a song while tying their shoelaces to get pumped up for their run.

One of my colleagues from New Zealand plays rugby. He does an amazing haka dance. You can immediately sense the energy from the moment he takes the squat position. We often ask him to show us the haka again. Haka was originally a Māori war dance to get warriors fired up, so he always needs a few minutes to calm down afterward. Rituals and routines can be potent ways to get into a state.

When our state matches the task, we are at our best. There are different states or different versions of ourselves that we need to call upon throughout the day. During your day, you might go from meticulously calculating a complicated project for a client proposal into a meeting with investors presenting a strategy, followed by a lunch meeting with an old friend you haven't seen in a while. At another moment, you find yourself helping your daughter with math, then stopping by your parents' place for a quick visit before picking up groceries at the supermarket (not forgetting anything), going for a run to decompress, and maybe ending up at the end of the day on your couch reading this book.

All these activities require you to bring different versions of yourself. A focused state that avoids making mistakes, an empathic state to make connections, a patient state doing routine chores, a calm state for introspection or creativity, an intuitive, sharp focus to address high-stakes situations, and so on. You aren't bringing the same version of yourself when you share a cocktail with a friend compared to addressing a board of directors. Nor will you freewheel across the myriad possibilities to solve a problem when you need to analyze numbers accurately.

By default, states linger whenever you need to bring a different version of yourself. Imagine you step into a brainstorming session with your team, having just got off a call in which you were told that you didn't get the deal you'd been working so hard on for the last few weeks. Or your son asks you to read him a bedtime story when you are working on an important presentation to deliver the next day. The level of attention you can bring to everything you do depends on your capacity to switch.

A lot of the switches we make throughout the day are done unconsciously. Routines we follow and habits we fall into automatically. Pouring the "I lost count" coffee before the next meeting. The deep sigh when opening our inbox. Checking our messages right before a meeting starts. Running these unconscious scripts that drag us through our days creates an energy-draining dissonance.

> *The level of attention you can bring to everything you do depends on your capacity to switch.*

The premise of a strong switch is becoming more conscious of our state and whether it suits an upcoming moment. Seeking out that version of yourself, the mood or mindset you feel is required to get the most out of a forthcoming moment, allows you to "switch on" for the moment. It makes that moment more valuable. By switching into it, space is made for the moment to exist. You basically allow the moment in its entirety to become part of your life.

This deliberate act of switching has a tremendous effect on your environment. You bring your attention and energy to the moment; people immediately sense you are switched on. You will be more in tune with them and with any shared content.

Making conscious switches brings a lot of powerful presence to your moments. Whether you are practicing meditation, performing on stage, leading a meeting, competing in a game, or writing a book, deliberately making the switch to get into the right state for the activity will make a massive difference to the experience and the outcome. **It is the simplest and most powerful tenet of the five**. Without a strong switch, the other tenets will have no effect on making space. The switch is your promise and dedication to making space.

THE POWER OF THE SWITCH

We don't go out for dinner as much as we used to. Since my wife and I transformed our garden into a permaculture-esque food forest, we are more conscious about the origin of the ingredients on our plates. Lately, we've often felt disappointed at restaurants, overpaying for food that wasn't sourced locally and certainly not organic. After COVID, prices seemed to have doubled while quality was far from improved.

But today, I felt like having an entertaining dinner with my family. We collectively decided to go to a Thai restaurant because we loved our family holiday to Thailand so much last year. We'd indulged in the fantastic culinary treats for an entire month. Spirits were as high as possible during the drive to the restaurant. It was an ideal moment to introduce a new "family" concept.

My wife has her favorite podcasts to listen to in the car. Most of them are food-related. Recently, she told me she learned about the beneficial effect of gratitude on the digestive system. Appreciating the food you are about to eat improves how your body processes it. I guess that is where "saying grace" comes from. I have encountered similar theories, which have always made much sense to me. The parasympathetic response of our autonomic nervous system is also called the "rest and digest" state. Our digestive system is susceptible to stress. Emotions of gratitude and appreciation are associated with safety and security – if we feel okay emotionally, our energy can be fully used for nourishment. Therefore, how you eat is as important as what you eat. Taking a moment to appreciate what you eat helps you slow down and enjoy every bite. Sharing the moment with others amplifies the appreciation. It creates the best state to ingest your food optimally.

"So … I was thinking …" I start, and my oldest son responds, "Here we go again." I had him particularly in mind when I started thinking about a gratitude practice to kick off our dinners. While my youngest son finishes his plate every time, including all his vegetables, my oldest leaves the vegetables untouched and rarely finishes his plate.

I continue, "Mom and I were talking about trying out something every time we have dinner together. We have learned how our bodies get a lot more good things out of our food if we like what we eat. Maybe we can take turns and talk about what we like about the dinner we are about to eat. I mean, at each dinner, someone different says something, so it remains fun and fresh?"

My oldest son replies, "I can't do that with every type of dinner because I don't like everything. I'll do it when we eat pizza." The youngest one seems to agree with the experiment, and I suggest we kick it off today at the restaurant.

Our appetizers are served, and I take a moment to share my memories of our past holiday in Thailand. "It is such a nice moment to spend together indulging again in the amazing symphony of vibrant flavors, combining the aromatic spices of lemongrass, ginger, and garlic with the tantalizing heat of chilies, balanced by the sweetness of coconut milk and the freshness of herbs like basil and cilantro, a culinary masterpiece dancing on our taste buds."

It was the first time, so I overdid it a little bit.

"It makes me think about the amazing places we have been together and the good times we have shared. This food this evening is a celebration of that. I love all of you and hope you will enjoy this as much as I will. I will savor every bite." I get smiles and nods around the table as everyone digs into their yummy plates.

I didn't expect it to have a long life. But then, the next day, my oldest son spontaneously took the floor and made a nice speech about how he really appreciated my effort to cook this nice dinner and hoped everyone would also appreciate it because he noticed me working hard in the kitchen to make it happen. We didn't have pizza, but it involved French fries, which may have motivated him to speak spontaneously. He added that he was planning to eat all the vegetables on his plate, but certainly not more than those on his plate.

The next day, my wife spontaneously spoke words of appreciation. It caught on.

The effect was amazing – and it shows the power of the switch. This appreciative switch focused our attention on the effort it took to prepare dinner and the time we spent together; it made the food tastier as we ate it with more care and attention. Evaluating the effect of switching together into having dinner, I can say, for one, we spend more time at the table now. Far more vegetables are consumed compared to before. More compliments about the food are given, and the atmosphere is generally better.

It might be because we are family, and we have probably built our own way of saying and doing things by now, but each "speech" since we started this ritual has a similar structure. It always begins with a sort of *why* we should appreciate the food. For example, it reminded us of a holiday; a lot of effort was invested; the ingredients were homegrown; or a family member passed on the recipe. The second part *connects us in the experience*, hoping everyone will enjoy it in the same way or pointing out specific things that are liked by any one of us in the moment. Finally, it ends with the "toastmaster" *sharing his or her intent*, expressing how he or she will eat the food. This became quite creative at times, with my sons expressing how they would mix up certain things, genius ways to fill up a tortilla, or chef-style approaches to garnish a pizza.

I recently came across an article explaining how famous sports coaches' pep talks are structured. To my surprise, they have a similar structure of *providing meaning, giving direction*, and *connecting with empathy*. This fantastic coincidence got me thinking about the best structure for a switch.

BUILD A SWITCH

Before outlining the different components of a good switch, let's first review what a switch is.

The SWITCH is a grounding practice to consciously invite in a moment and thereby commit to that moment.

> *To make space for a moment, we must first want the moment to happen.*

To make space for a moment, we must first want the moment to happen. The switch invites the moment. That means you let go of all resistance and allow this moment to happen. It is a practice of acceptance, a willingness to be part of the moment – a firm "yes," a deliberate decision to be part of it. Not only rationally but wholeheartedly wanting to take part. This unlocks a space for the moment to happen. Without the switch, there won't be a lot of space.

Resistance is also a source of stress. When you resist a situation, an event bound to happen, an unexpected statement or response from someone, or an uninvited incident, the gap between what you want it to be and what it is is the birthplace of stress. Tuning your "wanting" into the moment, taking away the resistance, is also taking away the possible tension.

The switch is the launch. It metaphorically refers to the energy of a take-off. The strength of the decision and the willingness to be part of this moment charge the space with energy. If you have a weak switch, you end up with a weak start to making space, which will easily close again with distractions. This grounding practice consists of three components. Together, these three components unlock space, inspired by the "pep talk" structure introduced in the previous section: 1) **inviting** the moment; 2) **embracing** the moment; and 3) **becoming** the moment. Like entering a room: you open the door, walk in, and take your place.

We invited the moment in at dinner by pointing out why it was so great to have this dinner together. We embraced this shared moment by connecting with the experience of enjoying the dinner, and by expressing our intention, we became part of the dinner. Space for experiencing the dinner together is now unlocked. Our attention is brought in, space is charged with our energy, and we can build this moment together, eventually becoming a nice memory in our treasure chest of cherished moments.

A powerful switch has a simple recipe. Open, walk in, and take your place. Invite, embrace, and become. I invite you to reflect upon your day and assess how many times you switched to open space for the moment to come into existence. How many times did you decide on a firm "yes" to the moment compared to how many times you didn't invite the moment in and just endured it, ready to move on from the start? How many meetings have you endured today? Wouldn't life be better lived if we practiced switching more often? Wouldn't our collaboration be elevated to co-creation if we practiced switching more consciously? Let's dig into these components of switching so we can start exploring the switch when collaborating with others.

> *Inviting the moment in is emotion-driven, not thought-driven.*

INVITE THE MOMENT

You cannot trick yourself into inviting the moment.

Imagine your mind says that you have to do this because it is part of your role, your job, your responsibilities, or people expect this of you, but your heart is saying you don't want to be in this moment because it feels like a waste of time. It may be an intimidating moment, or it triggers your anger or frustration. You are unable to switch. There will be no space unlocked for it. It will be hard for a valuable moment of co-creation to come into existence. You are not allowing it.

Inviting the moment in is emotion-driven, not thought-driven. If you try to generate an emotion of appreciation for this moment to happen and your critical mind keeps you from sincerely experiencing the appreciation, you cannot switch. It is a weak "yes," not a firm "yes." There are obstacles. There is resistance.

If you have a choice, you can decide not to come into the moment because the obstacles are too big for you to sincerely invite the moment. If you can't switch, it will waste your – and others' – time. There is also a lot of value in understanding why you can't switch, that is, what makes it hard for you to overcome the obstacles that keep you from pronouncing a firm "yes" to the moment.

If you don't have a choice or you really want to overcome your obstacles, there is growth ahead of you. Exploring different perspectives on the value of the moment and building your willingness to be part of it brings you closer to your switch.

It may just take a short reflection on what you are going to be part of and finding your heart in it; basically, framing it in the best way to consciously invite in the moment. Even if there are no obstacles, there is still much value in taking a moment to consciously decide to be wholeheartedly part of it.

EMBRACE THE MOMENT
You have invited the moment, and now you can bring your full attention to it. While the invitation points in the right direction, the embrace is the actual opening of space.

Attention is energy.

In quantum mechanics, observing a particle influences its behavior. This suggests that attention, in a quantum sense, can be considered a form of energy because it has the potential to interact with and influence the state of the things we focus on.

In energy psychology, attention is considered a form of mental energy that can influence the flow of energy within the body's energetic system. By directing attention to specific issues or emotions, individuals can facilitate healing and balance.

In Zen Buddhism, directing your attention with intention and awareness, you can tap into the boundless energy of the present moment and align yourself with the natural flow of life. In plain language, when you pay attention to something, you're giving it your mental energy and focus, just as a spotlight shines light and energy on whatever it lights up.

Embracing the shared moment is bringing your attention to other people and the situation. You are charging this moment with your attention. The potential of this moment, the potential for co-creation, is now growing. The more attention you bring to this moment, the higher the potential becomes and the deeper the space.

It is impossible to embrace the moment if you haven't invited it in yet. You can only walk in if you have decided to open the door.

Allowing your focus to converge on one thing at a time is the secret.

Embracing also means you are taking your attention away from other things. Bringing your attention to the moment can seem an easy task. What can make it more difficult is taking your attention and energy away from something else and trust things will still be fine. It takes a level of flexibility to become good at switching. Letting go of the urge to control the situation and allowing your focus to converge on one thing at a time is the secret of a powerful switch. You are concentrating your energy instead of diffusing it into multiple weak spotlights. By letting go, you free up your attention to be redirected.

If you have invited the moment but still have difficulty embracing it, you are not letting go of other distractions demanding your attention. Sometimes, it takes an agreement with others that you will not be available for a while or an agreement with yourself to ignore any distractions that could spontaneously occur.

> *Creation is born from intention.*

Bringing all your attention to the moment converges all your mental energy to this moment. It opens space for the moment to come into existence.

BECOME THE MOMENT
You have invited and embraced the moment. Now, it is time to become the moment by taking your place in it. The invitation points in the right direction; the embrace opens the space with your attention; and now you can become part of the space by setting your intentions clearly.

A firm "yes" and a strong presence are enough to be in the moment. More than just being in the moment, co-creation requires intention as well. In co-creation, we are creating from the unknown. Creation is born from intention. Your intention is your promise to yourself and the other participants. Without intention, everyone is merely present. Setting the intention activates all participants to become part of the moment. It is the final component necessary to complete the switch and unlock the space for co-creation.

Positive intentions within a group of co-creators create a resonance that uplifts and inspires everyone involved. It provides a supportive and conducive flavor to the space that helps turn collaboration into co-creation. When everyone feels invested, it bonds the group together and creates a sense of belonging. Each participant becomes more motivated to live up to their personal intentions.

The switch is now complete.

BIG SWITCH, SMALL SWITCH
Depending on the type of moment and the audience, the switch can happen as a swift conscious act or a very deliberate act requiring a bit more effort.

If everyone is familiar with each other and feels genuinely excited about sharing the moment, it will obviously be an easy switch for each participant. They were probably looking forward to engaging in this moment; it could even be the highlight of their day.

If it is a small moment, for example, you are meeting someone for half an hour, and there aren't any high stakes involved, the switch can also happen quite easily and rapidly.

If the shared moment is a high-stakes workshop with important big goals or the attendees have never worked together before, the switch might be a bit more challenging.

The same principles apply to both big and small switches. Each component in a big switch just needs a bit more intensity to be established.

In both big and small switches, a switch is done individually. You can only take care of your own switch. However, switching at the same time can bring the right level of intensity for big switches. For small meetings, every participant can take responsibility for their own switch. When I facilitate a large workshop, I find merit in taking some time at the start to allow everyone to make a synchronized switch. That way, I feel more confident about all the participants collectively making space for co-creation to happen.

I would like to evoke the "space maker" in you by presenting a range of practices to make a switch individually and synchronized in a group setting. Some of these practices have been tested and proven valuable; others have only been applied once. I would like to invite you to experiment as an individual and as a facilitator to build your own switch practices, opening space for co-creation.

SWITCH Experiments

PERSONAL EXPERIMENTS

The aim of the practices is to learn how to switch smoothly. Smoothness implies no friction, arriving quickly and easily in the state you want to be in. Your experimentation helps you discover your favorite ways to work through all three components. You will find knowledge below that turns into your wisdom by applying it in real situations. With some experimentation, your switch will become more natural and habitual. In no time, you will switch throughout the day, making space for each moment and getting better outcomes from more qualitative connections. You will be switching your way from collaboration to co-creation.

As an introduction to the practice, let me first explain what it looks like when I put the switch into action for myself.

MY PERSONAL PRACTICE
I practice switching as much as I can, but not all the time. I don't switch to go to the supermarket or the car wash. I tend to intuitively switch whenever I feel like the moment matters to me. I always switch when spending time with someone privately and in a work situation. I have made it a conscious act to switch when a moment of collaboration presents itself that I want to elevate to co-creation. I believe strongly in the value of charging the moment to allow for a level of synergy between minds that renders greater outcomes. Even if it is more of a random topic and a short get-together. The best insights arise from the most unexpected moments.

For example, what does a switch look like when I come out of a morning of calls and emails and have a meeting with a couple of people that will hopefully lead to a new opportunity?

"Open"
- I take a few minutes to close my eyes and check whether my mind is racing from dealing with the morning activities.
- I try to calm my breathing and let the thoughts come in and flow out of my mind.

"Walk in"
- If any thoughts have more weight than others, pulling on my attention, I let them continue, breathing out and bringing up a feeling of freeing myself of them.
- I imagine the upcoming meeting and the people, and I try to connect with what I appreciate so much about this meeting. The fact that they are taking the time to explore the opportunity with me makes me feel grateful. I don't take it for granted.
- I amplify that feeling of appreciation. The adventure of not knowing what is around the corner, the opportunity to connect with others, and the serendipity of it all help me amplify a feeling of gratitude. That feeling is the essence of my switch; it charges the space with energy.

"Take my place"
- That feeling also makes me want to set my intentions for the meeting. I will try not to be the one filling up all the space with my talking, and I will genuinely practice curiosity about what makes them tick and what makes them excited.
- I hold on to that sincere and open version of myself for a few seconds.
- I feel ready for this meeting. My switch is complete.

This is just a random example. It takes me no longer than two minutes. Sometimes, it takes me about five to ten minutes to switch. This happens when there is more resistance.

For example, when I have to facilitate a workshop, it takes me a bit longer to switch. I find myself switching before the moment starts, and it continues when everyone is still settling into the space. I have a more introverted nature and, therefore, a natural resistance to spending time with a lot of other people, let alone leading them into complicated thought processes together. I often use a tapping technique to manage resistance as the workshop starts, and I make a heart connection with all participants at the start of the workshop (my virtual "heart hugs"). My switch is half the work of being a good facilitator. It gets me tuned into the audience, and it heightens my senses.

Sometimes, the three components of a switch just feel overly complicated for the moment that is about to happen. If it needs to happen really quick, I just focus on "embracing the moment." I will make sure I confidently let go of things that are going on in parallel; I consciously eliminate distractions and stir up those good emotions about the moment to fully charge it. Practicing this one component often will make it easier to include dealing with resistance and setting your intentions after a while.

It has also been the most challenging component for me. When I was in a phase in my life where it was hard to appreciate or see the things I could be grateful for, these emotions didn't come up on demand. It took some effort sometimes to let go of thoughts that didn't serve me in the moment, including emotions that pulled me down. I had to increase my willingness to find the perspective on the moment that made me feel good about it, including the people in it. The latter can be the biggest challenge.

For most of us, including my introverted self, other people can be the hardest to deal with. But it is worth the effort to find the reason to appreciate them and amplify those emotions. <u>Collaboration does not turn into co-creation if there is no creative energy. There is only space for co-creation if you can find a heart connection with other people.</u> If not, it will be a rational meeting run by logical thinking alone, repeating what is known and mostly reinforcing control.

Now, let's break it down into pieces so you can rebuild it into the type of practice that works for you.

COMPONENT 1: *Invite the moment*

Your goal is to remove any resistance to the moment. It might be a catch-up, a workshop, a team meeting, a brainstorming, a one-to-one, or any other event about to happen.

A. INTROSPECTION
− Amplify the emotion(s) you have related to this moment.
− If negative, identify the key trigger. Is it lack of time, the people involved, the topic, or something else?
− If positive, identify what you like most and move on to the next component.

B. OPTION 1: Discharge the negative emotions by tapping
The emotional freedom technique, or EFT, inspires this. It is a technique related to acupuncture that works with acupoints. The practice suggested here is inspired by a part of the full method. You can find more information about EFT in a wonderful book written by Dawson Church called *The EFT Manual*.
− Create your setup statement:

Even though I … (negative trigger) …, I deeply and completely accept this moment.

For example:
Even though I am behind schedule and really need the time (=trigger), I deeply and completely accept this moment.

- Express your statement out loud or in your mind and observe the emotions.
- If the statement doesn't trigger the emotions, reconsider the wording of your trigger.
- Express it again to check whether it triggers the negative emotion.
- Repeat the statement a couple of times while tapping the side of your hand.*

*Use two fingers from one hand to tap the side of your other hand (the fleshy part under your pinky) as if tapping on a table. Not too hard and not too gently. The side of your hand is the part you would use to chop a brick in half using karate.

As you empathically repeat your statement and tap on your karate chop (KC) point at the same time, try to sense any release of tension.

The effects of tapping on the KC point vary from person to person. Some people feel immediate relief from emotional distress, while others may notice gradual improvements, practicing consistently over time. Tapping on specific points is still a subject of ongoing research, but many practitioners report positive outcomes in managing stress, anxiety, pain, and other emotional issues. Often, the key to success is finding the specific statement that releases stress by tapping on the KC point.

B. OPTION 2: Discharge the negative emotions by breathing

This is inspired by breathwork techniques documented by multiple authors. Breathwork has become popular over the past years. There are many sources of information available. My favorite breathwork expert is Dan Brulé. You can find more information about breathwork in his book *Just Breathe*. A sample exercise is the following:

- Sit up straight and relax your shoulders.
- Bring up the emotions related to the moment (your negative trigger).
- Become aware of your breath, particularly the effect of your emotions on your breath.
- Breathe in and out more deeply through your nose a couple of times while remaining aware.
- Breathe four counts in.

- Hold for seven counts as if you are gathering all those negative emotions in a bundle.
- Slowly exhale your bundle of emotions out of your system for eight counts.

As you breathe out, enjoy a pleasant humming or sighing sound if you can. An extended exhale triggers your parasympathetic nervous system and activates your vagal nerve (double activation with sounds like humming or sighing), thereby calming you down while removing those negative associations to the moment.

Repeat the cycle five to ten times to experience the full effect of the breathing technique. As with tapping, the outcome is highly affected by the emotions being triggered. If there is almost no resistance to work through, it will be more of a quick routine exercise. If there is a good amount of resistance with some strong emotions attached, the outcome of inviting the moment only happens if the exercise is done with full attention on your bodily sensations.

IN SUMMARY
This first step is detecting whether there is any resistance to the moment and if so, identifying the source of the resistance. The switch is all about "loving what is," and so both options help you deal with the negative emotions that keep you from switching into the moment. Both options are based on mainstream practices that have gained popularity in recent years.

We have opened the door. Now, let's walk in.

COMPONENT 2: *Embrace the moment*

Your goal is to let go of anything that might distract you from the moment and direct your attention to those who are part of the moment.

CONSCIOUSLY CLOSING OFF ALL DISTRACTIONS
- Assess any notifications across devices that may interrupt you.
- Assess any loose ends that might need your input during the moment.
- Do whatever is necessary to let go of these potential attention grabbers.

Although it is part of Component 2, this "closing off all distractions" aspect of the experiment might also happen before practicing any of the elements described in Component 1. Consciously organizing yourself to eliminate any distractions or worries allows space for the moment and gets you in the right mindset to embrace the moment. Next to inviting the moment, this is the second step of completely accepting what is. When you trust that everything has its own time and place, and things will also work out if you don't keep them continuously in check, you are converging your attention into a laser focus to bring it into the moment. All the distractions you allow will weaken your level of attention in the moment and make the space less deep.

HEART CONNECTION
Embracing the moment means embracing all the people in the moment. There is no room for judgment. Judgment keeps you from embracing the moment fully. In my experience, this is always the most challenging part in work environments. The stakes are high; people tend to identify with their roles and status; not everything that happens is fair; and personalities don't always naturally blend well together.

The following technique is inspired by heart coherence techniques made popular by the Heartmath Institute, established in 1991 in California.

Before you apply this technique, remember that practicing techniques like this genuinely makes you a nice person. I understand that not everyone can relate to "softer" practices, but everyone wants to be nice. With this in mind, I hope you are open to the following practice:
- Close your eyes.
- Slow down your breathing to five counts in and five counts out.
- Focus on your heart area (Optional: put your hand on your heart).
- Stir up the appreciative emotion related to being part of the moment.
- Direct this feeling toward the other people and the shared moment.
- Amplify it as much as possible from your heart area (Optional: visualize this feeling as a growing sphere coming from your heart area).
- Let go of any invading distracting thoughts; let them flow out again.
- End with the narrative, "This is where I am supposed to be and who I am supposed to be with; I happily allow space for anything that needs to surface in this moment."
- Open your eyes: you are good to go.

Less tangible as an experience, this heart coherence practice is, however, what "charges" the moment. Your state induced by this heart coherence practice will enable co-creation in the moment. You have opened space for deep connection.

IN SUMMARY
Consciously letting go of everything that might steer your attention away

from the moment is an act of commitment. Focusing on the heart area and cultivating positive emotions facilitates deeper emotional connections and enhances your relationships with others.

The heart is a vital organ responsible for circulating blood and oxygen throughout the body. However, scientific research has also shown that the heart communicates with the brain and other systems in the body through neural, biochemical, and electromagnetic pathways. Priming yourself for deep connection with techniques like heart coherence helps you embrace the moment with the people in the moment.

You are opening space by walking into it. Now, it is time to take your place. Then, the switch will be complete.

COMPONENT 3: *Become the moment*

Your goal is to step up to the plate now that you have decided to invite and embrace the moment.

A. BECOMING

"Becoming" is a lovely word that has gained significant recognition due to the memoir written by former First Lady of the United States, Michelle Obama. It carries connotations of growth, improvement, and the pursuit of authenticity and fulfillment, making it a powerful and evocative term.
In this context, I would like to use it to reference this first part of "Become the moment", which is about getting in touch with your best version of a team player. Here's how:

– Remember the last time someone sincerely appreciated something you'd done for them.
– Imagine that moment specifically and bring up the feeling of how you felt, particularly in terms of what motivated you to do this act for them.
– If this is hard, imagine the last time you had a great interaction with someone and bring that person alive again in your mind.
– Use the memories and related emotions to become the version of yourself you were in that moment with that person.

B. OPTION 1: Visualize

– Hold on to that image of yourself.
– Bring it into the upcoming moment.
– Visualize yourself acting and feeling like that version of yourself.

- Imagine visually how people will enjoy interacting with you.
- Imagine visually how you are contributing to this shared moment.
- Imagine visually how you will enjoy being exposed to their thoughts and creativity.
- Imagine visually how they will enjoy your ideas.

B. OPTION 2: Affirmations

Create a statement about who you want to be in the moment based on your "becoming" exercise.

For example:
"My energy fosters a positive and empowering environment where everyone feels valued, heard, and inspired to unleash their creativity. By bringing all my attention and listening deeply, I make people feel safe and valuable, fueling synergy and collective success."

You can write your affirmation down as a reminder or repeat it a couple of times until you know it by heart. An affirmation only works with empathic repetition, stirring your emotions every time it is repeated.

TRIGGER

Setting your intentions is one thing. It is another to act on them. Being guided by your intentions in everything you do requires internalization of these intentions. I am guessing that your intentions, the person you want to be in a shared moment of collaboration, might not be very different each time. I had internalized my intentions to be a certain type of person in collaboration by associating a "Pavlovian" trigger that helped me get into the right mood and mindset. It worked for a while, and then it wore off.

It was a kind of accidental programming that started a couple of years ago when I was participating in a very enjoyable strategy brainstorming session. For some reason, everything added up: the location, the timing, the people, and the vibe were perfect. We came up with entirely new perspectives on the future and identified opportunities that excited all of us. Everyone was on fire. We were in a delightful group flow state for a while. Out of nowhere, a "whistle" came out of my mouth whenever a great idea found its way out of someone's mind onto the table. I couldn't help it and didn't know what set it off. Did I hear someone whistle like this in a movie the other day? Did I pick it up somewhere else? It surprised me and even slightly embarrassed me the first time the whistle came out. Sometimes, you say something or make a certain sound that comes out quicker than you realize. It is a very odd phenomenon. People didn't seem to mind. I even noticed some smiles. It was a spontaneous "excitement whistle." Translated into words, it seemed to mean, "Wow, that's awesome!"

I associated the whistle with that great moment of co-creation. Afterward, I used it again and again, and for a while, it brought up the same feeling I'd had during the workshop. It got me in the right mood to co-create. It gave me a good feeling about the moment I was in and brought out the best version of myself to collaborate.

Whenever you are part of a great shared moment, and you feel you want to hold on to the version you are at that point, you can try to install a trigger – something that is very recognizable. It happens naturally with scents and often with songs. If you have a memorable moment or even a memorable time, for example, on holiday, and you are wearing a particular perfume, the scent will bring up all the feelings again if you smell it a couple of years later. If a great song is played throughout the summer, and you are having a great time, listening to the song after a couple of months or years will bring up that feeling again. The whistle did that for me.

It is worth experimenting with creating your own trigger whenever you are in the right state and the moment feels great.

IN SUMMARY
Removing any resistance to the moment and letting go of distractions to bring your attention completely into it opens the space for it to happen. By finding the version of yourself that matches the moment you are taking part in. Your intentions bring this moment to life for you. You are part of the created space that is full of potential. Bringing your attention to the space is only walking in. Bringing your intentions to the space is taking your place in it to become part of the moment.

GROUP EXPERIMENTS

Switching in a group setting feels totally different. You have to take into account the work culture.

The simple act of closing your eyes is easy when you are alone, but many people feel awkward closing their eyes in a group setting, especially a formal group setting. In a formal group setting, participants are often identified with their title or role. They bring their "work" version of themselves while they are completely different people on the tennis court or at family reunions. This means you can't "switch" in the same way you would when you're alone. Nevertheless, a group switch can still be very powerful in opening space for co-creation.

In a group setting, everyone is ready to start collaborating. There is less appetite for focusing on preparing to collaborate. Some might feel they are fully prepared and, above all, are not prepared to waste a lot of time on other things.

The switch becomes more of a ceremonial reminder compared to the conscious three-component act in a personal setting. That sounds like it loses its strength. It doesn't necessarily. You have the advantage of the energy of the group. If you have multiple people focused simultaneously on something, it multiplies the energy something receives – the magic of the force multiplier.

As a facilitator of a meeting, of a workshop, or of just the switch in a meeting or workshop, you are experimenting with concepts that help people invite, embrace, and become the moment, or all three, at once. It is a matter of understanding the culture and becoming creative in terms of helping them switch without making them switch off because your concept is too uncomfortable for them to act out.

The following are some concepts that have worked with different groups in different industries on different types of occasions. I didn't blindly apply the concepts. It was necessary first to understand the culture I was working in, ensuring they wouldn't upset or bore anyone.

Hopefully, these concepts will inspire you to develop your own skills in your role as a facilitator. Sometimes, the best way to invent the most suitable switch concept is to start from the culture and their shared interest areas and let this inspire you to develop the right switch activity. In a creative industry, you can have them visualize the ideal moment by drawing something. In a more formal financial or legal industry, you can have them come up with one or two competencies everyone in the group shares, which has the potential to make this collaboration exceptional. In a typical service or care industry, you can ask them to recall one of the most powerful moments of service they delivered and bring this feeling and this version of themselves into the shared moment. Your switch should help them with "wanting" this moment to happen. That is what opens the space for it.

INSPIRED BY TAI CHI

The switch can be acted out as a way of movement. As with Tai Chi Chuan, movement can embody a flow of energy brought into a moment. For instance, the group can stand up straight, close their eyes, move their arms in front of them with their palms facing each other, imagining they are holding their attention like a ball of energy. After a couple of breaths, they can lower their arms as if gently bringing their energy or attention completely into this moment, ending the exercise by sensing the space with the others in the group and finding their place among them.

Although it is a very simple gesture-like activity, it certainly is not within the comfort zones of people across corporate cultures. As an alternative, you can ask everyone to think about playing their favorite sport, and specifically, that moment where they need to step up and perform. For example, right before you serve in tennis, right before you kick a free kick in football, right before you hit with the bat in cricket or baseball. If the participants don't play any sports, they can imagine any moment in their life where they were about to perform; it could also be theater or spoken word. Have them take a few minutes to really relive that moment. This is the kind of attention that the co-creation needs. Ask them to repeat this visualization exercise regularly to get them back into the same state of focus. Until it wears off.

INSPIRED BY THE "CLENCHED FIST"

I read about the Clenched Fist in the book *I May Be Wrong* by Swedish economist, lecturer, and Buddhist monk Björn Natthiko Lindeblad. The idea is that people bring to mind all the things that have been keeping them busy that day, all the critical things demanding their attention. As they bring this to their minds, they must firmly hold on to these thoughts while clenching their fists. When ready, they will open their hands together and release these things, feeling confident that there is a place and time for everything. Now is the time to come into this moment, joining this group, setting the intention to make the most of this shared time with their full attention.

INSPIRED BY COHERENCE BREATHING

Coherence breathing or homeostasis breathing is a calming breathing that brings balance to the heart, lungs, and circulation. This state of balance or coherence is perfect for practicing heart connection with the rest of the group, inspired by practices from the Heartmath Institute. You will often find this element of heart focus while breathing in and out of the heart area in guided meditations. It is particularly interesting to combine it with a sense of spaciousness, which helps everyone get into a more creative state.

INSTRUCTIONS FOR THE GROUP:
- Straighten your back, relax your shoulders, and close your eyes.
- Inhale and exhale for a count of approximately five seconds.
- Concentrate on a feeling of appreciation in your heart area (opening the door).
- Visualize the expansion of that feeling of appreciation further with each exhale.
- Imagine it spreading across the room toward all participants (walking in the room).
- Bring the sense of appreciation back to your own heart.
- Savor the potential for each person to contribute meaningfully (taking your place).
- Sense the energy in the room.

When visualizing the expansion of the appreciative emotion in the room, I often ask the group to also visualize how it connects all the hearts of all those present. This may sound like a strange request for some groups, while others go with it enthusiastically. It is up to you to judge what fits best with your group. If you can have them connect their hearts during a breathing exercise and they are willing to engage with it completely, it will create a strong bonding moment that charges the room with creative energy.

Movement and breathing are great ways to induce the switch among participants. But this isn't often common practice in formal or corporate environments and can even create the opposite effect of generating anxiety, boredom, or even shame when it is too far outside the participants' comfort zone.

INSPIRED BY EXPOSURE THERAPY

As an alternative, ideal for formal environments, the switch can be realized by triggering reflection among participants using key questions and, possibly, visualizations. For example:

– When was the last time you gathered people together in co-creation?
– Can you envision the kind of person you wish had been present in that moment?
– Can you choose to embody those qualities in yourself?
– Do those desired traits align with what you value in others?
– Will you seize this moment to be that appreciated person?
– Could you create a small drawing, symbol, shape, or word art representing this version of yourself?

TASK: Fold the drawing and keep it in your pocket. It will remind you of the person you want to be for this moment. You will be reminded whenever you accidentally put your hand in your pocket.

In essence, the switch is personal. An individual can switch, but as a group, you can share the switch, which makes it more powerful. It charges the space, and literally the room, with the energy necessary for co-creation.

This chapter explained the switch as the first tenet. It is also the most powerful tenet. Without a switch, there is no use for the other tenets.

Dear Diary,

Reality hit. The project I always wanted to lead was assigned to me. I was overly excited about the opportunity at first. My excitement quickly turned into being overwhelmed and stressed. There are so many stakeholders involved, and it is hard to stay within the budget and timeline. I noticed my new superpower of making space faded a bit while getting lost, like a sock in a dryer trying to get the project on the rails. There is a lot on my mind, and it is hard to make space to find the treasures in collaboration with others. I did try something new today, though. There is hope. I had a high-stakes meeting with an important supplier for the project, and to make sure it went well, I took 10 minutes out for myself to get "in the zone" right before it happened. I was a bit intimidated by what was at stake in the meeting, but I turned it around by thinking about how great it would be if the meeting went my way. I also envisioned the best friendly, non-threatening, warm version of myself, deeply connecting with the others and holding the space for them to open up. She came to play in the meeting, and it worked well. I walked in without any resistance, and they picked up my vibe; we hit it off immediately from the start. I was able to bring my full attention and my best self, and it paid off. I might experiment a bit more with that "getting in the right frame of mind" practice for other meetings. It might just help me to not get too overwhelmed with the project so I can keep making space to connect with the other people, making sure we get the most out of our collaboration. I'm a work in progress, having a few glitches for character, still on my way to greatness, and taking a few wrong turns for fun. If I can keep front and center why each step along the way matters to me, I can juice up the energy and optimism to stay open and flexible in synergy with my allies. I guess that's all that matters. It needs to matter again and again.

Your Vaganaut

CHAPTER 4.
THE HOOK

WE MAKE SPACE for something when we have a compelling reason to shift our attention away from other things. All the distractions, marketing messages, social media messages, work-related messages, etc., and all the demands made upon us by our boss, children, partner, friends, and ego compete for our attention. What gets our attention depends on the strongest "pull." The hook.

PURPOSE VS. HOOK

Countless job satisfaction surveys indicate that people seek meaning in their work. Purpose is an important driver for people, creating in them a sense of some level of impact. Yes, people need to know their work matters.

I have seen cultural campaigns organized around the topic of purpose by human resource (HR) departments. Posters of happy employees on the walls everywhere. Beautifully written cases of how a given organization is impacting the world and thus creating pride among its workforce. Big goals and big aspirations moving everyone, or so it is assumed. How could all those people not care? Yet, these campaigns rarely move the "meaning" needle in job satisfaction surveys.

People often have difficulty understanding how their daily contributions can have a real impact. Big organizational achievements or goals don't make a hard-working, politics-facing, role-entitled individual feel significant.

All of us want to make an impact and be motivated. When taking on a job, we want to feel our work matters; *we* matter. We ask ourselves, "How can we make an impact?" to find the meaning in our work that motivates us. We rarely ask, "How does this impact me? How can this matter to me?" It would be a better question to ask, to find motivating meaning. We look for motivation by trying to understand how we can make an impact. But we are most often motivated when we understand *how something impacts us*. When do you really know you are having an impact? You would have to understand the perspective of the people you are trying to impact to answer the question of how something impacts you. Answering this question can get you hooked compared to trying to find your drive because of your purpose or impact.

> *We are most often motivated when we understand how something impacts us.*

With all the focus on purpose, it surprises me there is so little focus on creating hooks. Despite big goals that should provide a sense of purpose by stating the Big Why behind doing something, people still ask, "Why should this matter to me?" when asked to collaborate. To kick off an engaged collaboration, it is more productive for the participants to ask themselves, "In what way could this matter to me? In what way could this matter to us?" Even the facilitator can explore how the topic of the gathering can matter to each participant. Understanding the fragility of space and the competition for everyone's attention, exploring how the topic matters to each participant should be higher on the agenda than stating the overall purpose.

Imposing "non-cascadable" and often even meaningless (on a personal level) purpose statements makes people ask, "Why should this matter to us?" By making it a habit to look for the hook, people will start asking the explorative question, "How can this matter to me?" instead. Finding their own "pull" to keep their attention on the collaboration turning into co-creation.

THE CALL OF NATURE
I need to go. My dog needs to go as well. We both need to go. Nature is calling us. She literally needs to go. I just need to go for a walk in nature. These days, it is almost daily. A daily dose of nature. I didn't feel this longing for nature so intensely in the past. Getting older, I've become more and more hooked on spending time in nature.

She is staring at me. Something is about to happen. Could it be what she has been waiting for all morning? I say the magic word "W-A-L-K." She already knew when she heard the "W-A." It was enough to get her going. She is running up and down, making crazy doggy sounds, which probably translates into "I wrove you." I take my coat and the leash, and off we go.

Our street ends at the border of a natural park full of ponds and birds– mostly ducks, geese, swans, and likely some rare species. I often see birdwatchers lying on their bellies in the grass, spying on some birds with their long-focus lens cameras. They remain as still as possible, and my dog passes by, barking like crazy, pulling the leash to chase the birds. It's quite embarrassing.

We just passed the crossing from our street into the park and are now immersed in nature. Sounds of traffic are replaced by nasal geese honking. My cue to slide into a dreamy state, gazing at the horizon, giving my mind a break. Being surrounded by trees, water, and reeds is such a soothing feeling. I notice our dog, Roxie, overjoyed. She makes her way into the first pond. She enjoys bathing and drinking at the same time and makes a habit of doing this in every single pond we pass. There are a lot of ponds on this pathway, but strangely, it fosters my dreamy mood. I am instantly happy watching her enjoy our walk, and she often stares back at me with tons of gratitude in her eyes. We have walked down this path hundreds of times, but I notice something new each time. Every time, I discover a new element: a tree, a bird, a sound, or a mushroom. There is just so much variety if you are paying attention.

This small piece of nature takes up an important place in the life of every member of the family. It is where we go to take a break, relax, get our heads in the right place, have conversations and make decisions, and watch Roxie enjoy herself. I even come out here for a walk with people I meet with. I take calls while walking here.

When the call of nature is stronger, we take the car and drive out for an hour to Belgium's more foresty south to go for a hike. Nature has me hooked. And should I ask myself and the people who often join me in nature, "**In what way does nature matter to me?**", the answer is layered.

At the most general level, the hook of nature is all about beauty and its calming effect. This probably resonates with most people who like to spend time in nature. At a deeper level, the hook is about finding peace of mind and regaining perspective, which is easier when immersed in nature. At the deepest level, in the serenity of nature, I feel whole, inspired, and alive. Nature's embrace helps me shed the burdens of the world. In essence, it grounds me; it makes me a better person. Life's stressors have less power over me, and I become a nicer person to hang out with.

> *Deeper layers intensify the "pull."*

Just like nature has a hook for a lot of us. City life can also have a hook. Your hobbies have you hooked. Your interest areas have you hooked. These are things that somehow matter to you at this moment in your life. Your motivation doesn't come from the impact you could have; it comes from the hook, which is the reason it matters to you. Just like with this example of how nature got me hooked in multiple layers, the way you are hooked is layered as well. Deeper layers intensify the "pull." To find a strong hook that has a sufficient "pull" of our attention, we need to understand the layers of the hook.

A HOOK IS LAYERED

Everything in life has a story. Stories we tell ourselves and stories we tell others. Stories help us make meaning of life events. They drive our decisions and behavior. None of the narratives we create are completely true or completely false. They are subjective and evolve with our experiences in life.

Our stories are amalgamations of our beliefs, experiences, and emotions. They determine how much of something we allow or desire in our lives. They determine the amount of attention we invest in something. Our narratives are vessels for one or more hooks that pull our attention in certain directions. These hooks, just like our narratives, are layered. The top layer is general and often more rational. It is what we can easily tell other people. Deeper layers are more personal and replete with emotion. The deepest layers of why we get hooked on something are not always visible – even to us.

Our behavior can be driven by deep-rooted hooks. But we don't have to dig deep to find meaning.

> *This spirit of collectivity increases the pull for attention and makes space that lasts.*

The top layer usually provides the lightest level of meaning because it is often less personal. The way organizations talk about purpose usually touches on the top layer because purpose in this context needs to be relevant to all those involved.

Deeper layers are more personal and emotion-driven. They can be different from person to person. Emotions strengthen hooks. Emotions pull attention.

While "switching" is about "wanting" a moment to happen, the hook is about "sustaining desire" for a moment to happen. The hook keeps the space open by pulling attention in. Finding the right layer of the hook is an act of framing a topic in such a way that it matters, stirring emotion. A hook is a personal reason, but it can be shared or empathized with by others. Whenever people share or empathize with each other's hooks, they build trust in each other. Trust glues a group of people together into a collective. A collective emerges when there is a collective pull of attention into a moment. If trust levels are high, because the participants resonate with the hooks that pull their attention, they make space together. This spirit of collectivity increases the pull for attention and makes space that lasts.

THE PULL
The hook pulls our attention. The strength of the pull determines the level of attention and, therefore, the depth of the space made. We can increase the strength by framing our own hook well, at the right layers, and by nurturing a spirit of collectivity with *all* hooks.

> *The feeling of being drawn to the same thing connects us.*

The strongest pull doesn't come from the most generally framed hook that "makes sense" to everyone. Ironically, the most common denominator doesn't render the strongest connection between people. Just as a statistic tells you nothing about the motivation behind a behavior. It is averaged out, flattened. A strong stake connects people, yet it doesn't need to be the same stake to connect individuals. **The feeling of being drawn to the same thing connects us**. Not necessarily having the same reason to be drawn to something. The strongest pull comes from something that matters to you, amplified by knowing it also matters to other people for their own reasons.

The Macarena dance craze in the 1990s is a nostalgic example of how cultural phenomena, such as dance moves, can spread rapidly through imitation, especially in social settings where people observe the behavior of others. The feeling of sharing a similar interest, of being hooked on the same thing, connects people. And that kind of connection, that spirit of collectivity, makes them even more hooked. It provides social proof for the hook, strengthening it even more.

A personal, well-framed hook combined with a shared interest and the spirit of collectivity generate a strong pull to make space for a shared moment.

This would be the most important recommendation for HR departments in organizations. People connect because they share an interest. Not necessarily because the reason for the interest is the same. If you share the high-level, mainstream, big goal purpose as the reason why everyone should be connected to the organization, it would not be as strong as making visible how everyone is connected to the organization for their own reasons.

FRAMING A HOOK

We get hooked on something because there are aspects that resonate with us. Aspects that pull our attention. Triggers. These triggers get us hooked because a need gets fulfilled in some way. They touch upon our human needs. As mentioned before, a hook is layered. Each layer adds context to the triggers that hook us. The narrative of the top layer of a hook is generic. At deeper layers of the hook, our narratives become more personal and emotional, rendering us more vulnerable. Framing a hook for the strongest pull would need us to identify the most compelling trigger and identify how it touches on our needs. How it generates feelings that create the "pull."

To make the layers and related emotions more concrete, here is a fictional example of a layered hook in a job setting:

TOP LAYER
I am hooked on my job in this organization because we …
… empower people to live healthier, happier lives by providing innovative healthcare solutions.

MID (MORE PERSONAL) LAYER
I am hooked on my job in this organization because I …
… have experienced a lack of good healthcare solutions in my family. I have witnessed loved ones suffer because they didn't have access to proper treatments and support. They didn't have access to people with the proper knowledge and competencies to make their lives easier. Here, I am part of a team that builds innovative healthcare solutions that are available to anyone. Our approach is truly people-centric. Everyone deserves a life free of suffering.

DEEP (PERSONAL) LAYER
I am hooked on my job in this organization because I …
… have felt so powerless and useless witnessing loved ones enduring deep suffering while technology and science exist to relieve them of it. I want to believe in a world where everyone can live happily without suffering

– not just the privileged. The breakthroughs in our work make me feel that we matter for many people. We are changing lives for the better. I feel significant. It helps me deal with that feeling of powerlessness from the past by making significant progress every day.

The deeper the layer, the more it touches upon basic human needs. Our basic human needs drive our behavior. Great minds have discussed these needs in different ways throughout recent history. The best-known "hierarchy of needs" by Abraham Maslow lists physiological needs, safety, love/belonging, esteem, and self-actualization. Carl Rogers, a prominent humanistic psychologist, emphasized the importance of psychological needs, such as self-esteem, self-actualization, and positive regard from others in promoting personal growth and well-being. Edward L. Deci and Richard M. Ryan developed the self-determination theory (SDT), which states that humans have three innate psychological needs: autonomy, competence, and relatedness. In Daniel Pink's popular book *Drive: The Surprising Truth About What Motivates Us*, autonomy, mastery, and purpose are highlighted as the key intrinsic motivators that drive human behavior and performance. Tony Robbins, a motivational speaker and self-help author, identified six popular basic human needs: certainty, variety, significance, connection/love, growth, and contribution. All these interpretations of human needs have an angle of **self**, autonomy, mastery, and growth, as well as an angle of **self in relation to others**, love/belonging, safety, contribution, and connection.

Framing a hook to maximize its pull would need us to bring the three angles together: the most compelling *trigger* that catches our attention, the relation of it to *self*, and the *context* in relation to others. "The Hook Triangle." These three angles work in unison to create the hook. Using the triangle to frame a hook can happen on a more generic or deeper layer, digging to understand our basic human needs that create the pull.

Framing hooks with the hook triangle helps us become more conscious of what pulls our attention to a moment. And if we become more conscious, we can manage our attention better to make space. The triangle is an ideal way to frame our hook when we want to elevate the moment from collaboration to co-creation.

THE HOOK TRIANGLE
A hook has three angles: **the trigger, the self, and the context.**

The trigger is the aspect that catches our attention. It can be an insight, a realization, or a novel piece of information. It works as a cue to trigger our thoughts and emotions. Often, it is perceived as a big opportunity.

The self is about how we relate this **trigger** to ourselves. It resonates with our values, identity, and aspirations. It may just speak to us on a rational level and have an emotional appeal on a deeper level.

The context is about how this **trigger** and its relation to our **self** has relevance in a broader context. It is the positioning of our self in the world in relation to others. It is our social validation, the social proof that arises from observing similar behavior in others. It is the fear of missing out, of not belonging or not being up to par with common knowledge or competencies, not being respected, acknowledged, or loved. It can stir up emotions related to self-worth and companionship.

Not all hooks have the same depth, and each hook has its own "weight balance" across the three angles. Sometimes, you are hooked on something because it is fun and adds variety to your life. The trigger is a nicely designed, personal invitation to join in the fun, but it doesn't particularly speak to any of your deep-rooted values or principles. It just makes you feel good when you engage with it. It also builds your social currency, compares your skill level with others, and connects you to like-minded people in a community. For example, this could describe a hook to a game.

Another hook might not be triggered by such a novel, mysterious, intriguing, insightful, or loud and fun trigger. It could be a familiar and random trigger. But it touches upon your core values, your idea of who you are, and what you stand for. It might still be less contextual and have no impact on how you relate to the world. This could be a situation where your attention gets pulled into a conversation with your mother. The trigger is her telling you to take better care of your health, exercise more, or let go of bad habits. It could become more contextual if it stirs up emotions about how people might disapprove of you.

As another example, let's say you arrive at a restaurant and notice a group of your friends having a nice dinner together. This will probably not make you question who you are, what you stand for, or what your desired growth is as a person. It might make you question whether you are appreciated and loved or belong with this group because you were not invited. The trigger of seeing them sitting together is unexpected and novel, not repetitive nor very compelling in itself. A split-second trigger that hooks you into a long trail of thoughts about how you relate to this group of friends.

Exploring the kind of emotions, the strength of the feelings, and the angle from which they come helps to understand the pull of a hook. By framing the hook, it becomes top of mind and it becomes a great tool to consciously pull your attention to the moment.

HOOKS IN CO-CREATION

In the context of this book, hooks, as a concept, is not about forming habits or creating "contagious content." It is also not about understanding the deep-seated needs behind conscious or unconscious behavior; it is not therapy. In the context of this book, framing a hook is about managing our attention for better co-creation. Shaping our hooks ourselves and "hooking into" each other's hooks is an effective way to make deep space for a shared moment to come into existence. It primes us to stick with it for as long as necessary. It helps us win the attention competition with many other attention grabbers. Reminding ourselves of our hooks during co-creation pulls us back in when we wander off. Articulating our hooks in a compelling way uses the power of language to stir up emotions that keep us in the zone.

The hook triangle framework can help you identify and articulate the right hook for yourself. When you frame the hook as a triangle, you can see whether there is an emotional load and why. You can dig deeper when it doesn't feel like your hook moves you. You can also move up a layer when you feel it is becoming too personal and specific and losing its appeal to work on. As mentioned before, this is very subjective and, therefore, a personal exercise. I don't see many people consciously practicing this today to make space for co-creation. The hook triangle should make it easy to frame your hook in the strongest way. And sharing hook triangles can increase the spirit of collectivity. It is a powerful vulnerability exercise.

Let's make this very practical with personal and group experiments.

HOOK
Experiments

PERSONAL EXPERIMENTS

This practice aims to help you find and strengthen your hook with the topic of the moment so you can make space for it. It should help you answer the question, "In what way can this matter to me?" Asking this question any time you feel the need to pull your attention back into an upcoming moment will already deepen the space; it will help you experience the moment more consciously. You will be more present.

Let me start by giving you an idea of how I practice the hook before we break it down into more detailed guidance.

MY PERSONAL PRACTICE
Asking myself often, "In what way can this matter to me?" turns out to be very effective. It is another way of asking myself what stirs up my emotions. What is it about this upcoming moment that means something to me? Because I switched before, I am in a state of mind that I want this moment to happen. That state of mind helps me to find the answer to why I want this moment to happen.

My first thought is always a rational reason. For example, it can give me an answer that moves the project forward; it helps me understand what I need to deliver; it maintains a relationship that helps me in my work, etc. These answers usually don't result in a strong pull. I continue scanning what triggers me and where the emotional load is related to this moment. The desired outcome of the moment crosses my mind and gives a bit more substance to the reason I want this moment. For example, I want to understand how much they are bought into the idea and what level of support I can count on; I want to be inspired to try a new approach because I am stuck; I want to be recognized for what I have achieved and feel acknowledged for my capabilities.

The desired outcome is often the quickest way to find my trigger. It becomes harder if I am not quite sure of the desired outcome. In that case, I start scanning the kind of conversation I would like to have and what that could bring me. What is the biggest opportunity of the moment? This eventually leads me to some idea of the desired outcome. When this reveals the trigger and the reason why it matters to me, I start "layering." I try to figure out what's going on with this trigger. Am I looking to learn something, to be empowered, to grow, to work toward my aspirations? Is it driven by a value or by principles I feel strongly about? Am I also looking to get contributions from others, validation, a confirmation of an identity I personify with (the expert, the leader, the manager, the problem-solver, etc.)? That usually gets me to the right pull for my attention. For example, I figured out the moment allows me to use my best talents or it can give me a totally new perspective that helps me deal with the difficulties that keep me from feeling progress and success, I felt alone working on this challenge, and I have a chance to find some allies.

It can become a vulnerable and sensitive exercise finding the hook. I pay most attention to the layer that feels comfortable. There is no need to reflect on the deepest layers of my motivation to find motivation. Again, it is not therapy; I just try to figure out what moves me. What pulls me toward the moment. Once I have touched on it and I feel the related emotions, I am good to go. By feeling the related emotions, it becomes top of mind and easy to recall.

With the risk of overcomplicating the practice of framing triangles, let's break it down into smaller actionable bits so you can rebuild it in a way that works for you.

Note that everything you break down into details will appear more complicated than it is. Let the triangle just be a reminder to consider three angles when looking for your hook. What triggers you? Why does it trigger you? Does it stir up emotions because it matches with something you find important? Does it stir up emotions because it affects your relations with others? It is a simple reflection to find out what moves you; to make sure you have the handles to stay hooked for as long as you need to.

IN WHAT WAY CAN THIS MATTER TO ME?

Finding your hook starts with this key question. It is an explorative question and not a judgmental question. It is not questioning whether it can matter. It is a question asked to discover the strongest arguments to make it matter. It is a genuine exploration. A broad range of options can pull your attention to the moment, and they each have their own depth to explore. It is a horizontal (options) and vertical (depth) exploration that I like to call "Hook and Harmonize."

It doesn't make sense to hook and harmonize for a chat at the coffee machine or water cooler. The hook and harmonize is a practice you would apply when you are about to share a moment, and you feel it is appropriate and valuable to try and elevate it from mere collaboration to a level of co-creation.

Hook options (different triggers).

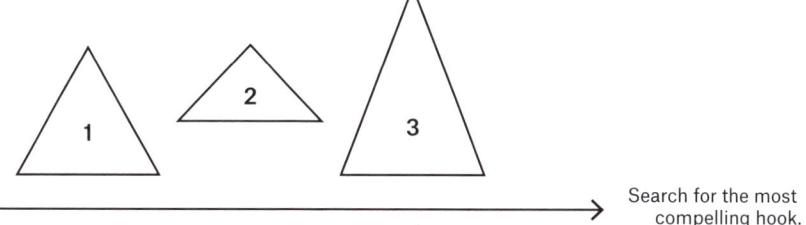

Search for the most compelling hook.

Harmonize (Layers of the hook, reflecting on self and context).

Search for the interpretation that provides the right pull.

Hook and harmonize: a horizontal and vertical exploration to find the right pull for attention.

HOW DO YOU FRAME YOUR HOOK?

The following three steps can be repeated a few times. There are probably several hooks to explore with different pulls for your attention. Follow your gut feeling and scan triggers of the moment that generate emotion. When the most compelling trigger(s) are revealed, harmonize to find the right pull. It doesn't need extensive exploration.

Step 1. Identify the trigger
TRIGGER: The aspect of the upcoming moment that stands out. It has the potential to stir up emotions from the angle of *self* or the angle of *context*. It might be the main opportunity brought by the moment that relates to self and is impacted by a broader context in relation to others.

A trigger that can sustain your attention in co-creation **is something you need at this moment**. It is something worth looking into.

Trick the trigger
If the trigger is hiding and you are having a hard time spotting it, you can trick it into revealing itself by asking the following questions:

- What might be an amazing outcome of this gathering – and why?
- What are the most interesting things others could bring to the table?
- What would our collective blind spot be?
- Which emotion would relate to this gathering – and why?
- What is the greatest contribution I could bring – and what effect might it have?
- Given all my knowledge and experience, what do I have no clue about regarding this topic?
- If we were all absolutely brilliant, what is the hardest thing we would solve first?
- Which aspect triggers the most intense emotions among us (participants at this gathering)?
- What is the strongest reason I don't want to do this gathering – and why?
- If I were excluded from this gathering, what would I miss out on, and what would the others miss out on?
- This is a marathon, and the meeting lasts for 24 hours; which is my topic of choice to spend the most time on?
- When you have found one or two triggers that match some of the criteria above, write them down separately with some space to add the other parts of your triangles.

Hook options (different triggers).

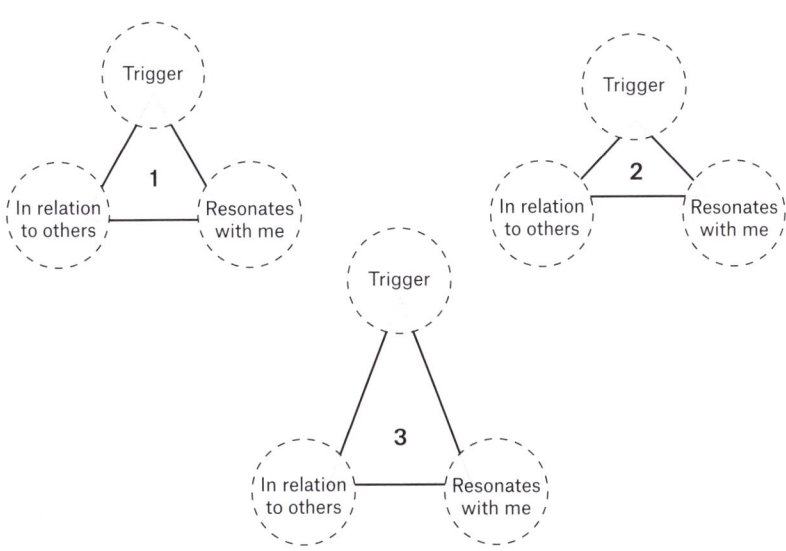

Examples of triggers
- "If we could find the common threads in our different messaging, we should be able to create one strong voice to the outside world."
- "If we get a good idea of what our customers are dealing with and under what circumstances every day, we might be able to construct a better setup to provide the right intel at the right time."
- "Opening up to our differences can bring us closer when things get hard."
- "This could give me a glimpse of how he came up with this amazing leftfield approach, helping me solve a similar problem."
- "Even if the ideas are conventional, I can uncover their thinking patterns when they brainstorm."
- "Sign-off or no sign-off, I can at least bring the proven risks to their attention."
- "Let me use this opportunity at our catch-up to understand his perspective, as well as the perspectives of his peers of the same generation, regarding these situations."
- "I have some curve balls planned to cause controversy. Let's see who dares to speak up and take the lead and who follows."

Triggers are those aspects that turn a gathering into a great opportunity. As mentioned before, they are worth exploring for several reasons. Why those reasons matter to you is often linked to self and context.

Step 2. How do you relate to the trigger? (Self)
The three angles of the triangle together form a strong hook. A trigger resonates with you only if you can relate to it and if it has an impact on how others relate to you. An easy way to reflect upon how the trigger relates to you is to investigate your thinking, doing, and feeling related to the trigger.

Think, do, and feel
Think, do, and feel is about your opinion and beliefs related to the trigger, your behavior related to the trigger, and how the trigger makes you feel.

Example:

SITUATION An upcoming meeting with management where you want to pitch a new approach that needs a significant amount of resources. This new approach is necessary due to a potentially significant problem arising in the future.

TRIGGER (the reason you want to have this meeting)
"Sign-off or no sign-off, I can at least bring the proven risks to their attention."

THINK (your opinion about this trigger)
"It is my job to warn them of any risky situations promptly. Management needs to be able to count on my expertise. In this way, I can help them anticipate problems, which benefits us all. Even if they don't agree with my sense of urgency, it is better to disagree and have the risks on their radar than not bring them to their attention."

DO (your typical actions or behavior)
"I always want to keep risky situations in check. By preparing some scenarios and clearly stating the consequences, I can make sure this is at the top of the agenda of all stakeholders. I'll also spread the word across the team with the help of my usual allies."

FEELING (the emotions triggered)
"I am excited about getting a window to showcase this future problem. Being hands-on about problems and immediately taking the bull by the horns makes me thrive. Like last time, I expect management to be attentive and make immediate decisions. That is what I love about my work. No BS, just seeing things the way they are and immediately dealing with them. It makes me feel that our work is significant, and we get better each day."
"**THE SELF**" angle is an exploration of how we relate this **trigger** to

ourselves. We want to understand how this trigger resonates with our values, identity, and aspirations. You can kick off this THINKING, DOING, and FEELING approach by just asking yourself why this trigger triggers you.

Step 3. What kind of context makes this trigger relevant?

Exploring the context of a trigger takes the "self" out of isolation. There is always a context that makes a trigger more relevant for you. A trigger becomes relevant by relating your THINKING, DOING, or FEELING to others. It might spring from past experiences, current situation assessment, or future scenarios.

PAST Your past perspective stems from your experience of sharing or disagreeing on opinions with others. Some people may have collaborated well with you in achieving goals. In contrast, others may not have supported your controversial new initiatives. Your memories of interactions with others in the past are associated with certain emotions.

CURRENT Your current perspective comes from observing the situation at this moment. Does the trigger also trigger other people? Do they share your opinions? How are they behaving in the moment in relation to the trigger? Do they seem to have the same goals? Can you empathize with their feelings related to the trigger?

FUTURE Your future perspective comes from your assumptions about people's opinions, behavior, and feelings, built on your past experiences and current observations.

Example (continued):

SITUATION An upcoming meeting with management where you want to pitch a new approach that needs a significant amount of resources. This new approach is necessary due to a potentially significant problem in the future.

TRIGGER "Sign-off or no sign-off, I can at least bring the proven risks to their attention."

THE THINKING SELF "It is my job to warn them of any risky situations promptly. Management needs to be able to count on my expertise. In this way, I can help them anticipate problems, which benefits us all. Even if they don't agree with my sense of urgency, it is better to disagree and have the risks on their radar than not bring them to their attention."

THE DOING SELF "I always want to keep risky situations in check. By preparing some scenarios and clearly stating the consequences, I can make sure this is at the top of the agenda of all stakeholders. I'll also spread the word across the team with the help of my usual allies."

THE FEELING SELF "I am excited about getting a window to showcase this future problem. Being hands-on about problems and immediately taking the bull by the horns makes me thrive. Like last time, I expect management to be attentive and make immediate decisions. That is what I love about my work. No BS, just seeing things the way they are and immediately dealing with them. It makes me feel that our work is significant, and we get better each day."

THE CONTEXT "I certainly don't want to be blamed for not pointing the risks out promptly. I don't want to be perceived as the cause of a crisis – as this is my responsibility. But it is highly unlikely. People respect me as the "rock-the-boat" kind of person and remember how that saved us last time when we were faced with a meltdown. They expect this of me. Management hired me to challenge them and be the spark for improvement. This is my moment to rally the believers behind an exciting project again and be recognized for the change agents we are."

This shows a complete hook triangle for an upcoming shared moment, including a description of what triggers your attention, three different descriptions of how it relates to self, and a description of the context in relation to others. All three angles, in unison, become the narrative that pulls your attention into the moment. It answers your question, "In what way can this moment matter to me?"

Note that there is no right or wrong way to practice this. Any way you arrive at a narrative that holds sufficient emotional load to pull your attention is a good way.

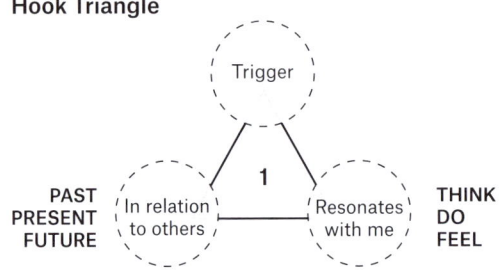

YOUR NARRATIVE

The hook triangle becomes your narrative, pulling your attention into the moment. It keeps the space open for the moment to come into existence. A strong narrative is important to make space. By consciously exploring your narrative, you become hooked into the moment.

We seek pleasure and try to avoid pain; we seek social acceptance and try to avoid social rejection. We want to have hope, not fear. Both seeking and avoiding drive our (often unconscious) behavior. If you consciously explore the narrative that works best for you to make space, it is important that the narrative is about seeking pleasure, social acceptance, and hope. It doesn't put you in the right state for co-creation to be motivated by a narrative about avoiding pain, social rejection, or fear.

It's equally important not to become overly attached to your personal narrative. There can be multiple triggers, each having a subjective relation to yourself and others. In other words, numerous ways exist to perceive a given moment's opportunities. Multiple valid reasons can demand your attention. There is no single correct interpretation. In this sense, there is no need to be consumed by your narrative. It can be beneficial to shift your attention to the present moment when your narrative seems overwhelmingly important. If you cling to it dogmatically, it becomes rigid and hinders collaboration. Remain an observer, using your narrative as a hook to make space.

HOW DO YOU HARMONIZE YOUR HOOK?

Now that you have explored your narrative for substance, it needs a final check to see if it is strong enough to make space for co-creation. We want to harmonize it, ensuring we are satisfied with the depth of the three angles. Does it really answer the question, "How can this move me?"

Example:

SITUATION An agency meticulously organizes a team day with specific activities to help a team bond on a deeper level. People aren't currently supporting each other or sharing things openly. There seems to be some underlying friction. This team day is designed to stir up some feelings of vulnerability and community. Let's harmonize the hook of a participating team member.

TOP-LAYER HOOK

TRIGGER "Opening up to our differences can bring us closer when things get hard during work."

SELF "I always organize informal moments with colleagues I need to work closely with to get to know each other more personally. It is the way to teamwork. It gives me a feeling of community and interdependency."

CONTEXT "All the colleagues, friends, and family with whom I had earnest conversations about our differences have become close and trusted people in my life. They also perceive me as trustworthy, and we often share very personal information with each other."

MID-LAYER HOOK

TRIGGER "If we can show a more vulnerable and personal side of ourselves, we will want to have each other's back in the future. Everyone will grow more attached to this team."

SELF "I will only show my vulnerable side if the others do, too. I am not a very trusting person and I think it is wise to be on guard in a work situation. Changing the environment and having the right activities will certainly help me let my guard down a bit. Especially when I experience the others in a different light."

CONTEXT "Letting my guard down in the past led to some disappointment with people I trusted. But then again, we never really tried to get to know each other this way. Work can become much easier and lighter-hearted if we all let our guard down and show vulnerability to each other. If one trusts the other, it is also easier for the other to trust. It should start somewhere, and this might be it."

DEEPER-LAYER HOOK

TRIGGER "If we change the environment and the activities, it will get everyone to stop playing these roles with each other, identifying with their title, status, or expertise."

SELF "I really feel uneasy in an environment where people don't say what is on their minds. The formal language we use when facing each other, but the contrasting informal conversations behind each other's backs, all these facades, make me feel lonely and threatened. I struggle to play my role well, as I often say things I shouldn't or fear saying something stupid. To feel comfortable in this team, I need to see past the facades and understand the genuine selves behind the people. Are they human as well?"

CONTEXT "When we talk with each other, there is never any emotion. It is all very rational, smart, and factual. When I show emotions, it feels out of place. Although some people have told me how much they love my sincerity, I don't feel my impulsive rants are always appreciated or seen as professional. I would love to see someone else laugh too loud, lash out, or do something irrational just so I feel more at ease being me. I don't want to filter everything I say all the time. It's exhausting."

In this example, we have a layered hook that shows a version of the hook at different depths. Finding the hook is a horizontal movement, browsing across triggers and exploring how we relate to them. Harmonizing the hook is the act of digging into the layers of the hook to explore which one feels right. It is deliberately called "harmonizing" because you are looking for harmony. The depth of the narrative should be just right to keep you hooked.

The DEEPER LAYER in the example might hit on something that really pulls your attention. It can make you excited about an improved future collaboration, removing some of your frustrations. It could also be that it feels too heavy to use as a hook. You might not completely resonate with it. You prefer to hook in with the MID LAYER because maybe it makes you less like a "drama-lama." Maybe the TOP LAYER is just fine. You are practical, and this hook resonates well with your hands-on approach. You don't need to stir up all kinds of personal emotions; you need the prospect of progress to keep your attention in check.

Exploring the deeper layers of a hook helps you experiment with its impact on you personally. That is why exploring the hook triangle to generate a narrative is an individual exercise. It is subjective and can be completely different for each participant.

GROUP EXPERIMENTS

Finding the right narrative to get hooked is a personal quest. Yet, it dramatically increases the strength of a hook if you share the practice with other people in a shared moment. As a facilitator of a co-creative session, you have three options to bring a group together in this practice and nurture the spirit of collectivity that will eventually help them take ownership of a topic. One, you can make suggestions in terms of exploring their personal narrative when inviting them to the session. You can also task them with creating a hook triangle in preparation for the session. Third, you can have them share their hooks and build a "spirit of collectivity" wall at the start of the session.

MEANINGFUL INVITATION

Whenever I try to plan a meeting with people, I notice agendas are more packed than ever. Especially when their agendas are open for colleagues to block time when they see an available spot. People invite people to meetings and even workshops without properly explaining why they are invited and what the planned outcome is. A lot of meetings even have the goal of figuring out the goals for the next meetings.

Whenever you want to get people excited about something you are inviting them to, you need to add one or more hooks to your invite – aspects that help them see the magnitude of the opportunity that comes with getting together. You can use a strong quote from a respectable person, an anecdote that brings it to life, a surprising statistic, or even a provocative statement. Adding a good hook that pulls their attention to the moment you are organizing is respecting their time investment when they have so much going on. They deserve some help understanding why the time you're requesting is more important than the time they could invest in another meeting, project, or even time with family.

By adding interesting hooks to an invitation, you are also helping your invitees create their own triangles and narratives.

Example:

SITUATION You have organized a meeting with a couple of colleagues from other departments who recently completed a project successfully. They had the same challenge your team is currently facing. They will present the full project to your team in this meeting.

INVITATION HOOK To capture your team members' attention and hint at a personal hook they might explore when sending them an invite, you add this quote from Steve Jobs, the co-founder of Apple, Inc.

> *"Innovation comes from people meeting up in the hallways or calling each other at 10:30 at night with a new idea, or because they realized something that shoots holes in how we've been thinking about a problem. It's ad hoc meetings of six people called by someone who thinks he has figured out the coolest new thing ever and who wants to know what other people think of his idea."*

In your invitation, you continue by explaining how you see this as an ad hoc inspirational sharing to nudge us out of our conventional thinking about an issue. And you add the question:

> *"When did a novel solution ever come from the same thinking in your work?"*

By adding this quote together with a provocative question, you are adding a hook to your invitation that will help pull the interest and attention of your invitee to the moment of the gathering. It may trigger your invitee and stir up an emotion related to how important it is to inspire each other and share best practices. It might kickstart a narrative in their minds that hooks them to this meeting.

It becomes a meaningful invitation, suggesting good reasons to pay attention.

HOOK AS HOMEWORK

As a facilitator, I have tasked workshop participants with preparing a hook triangle as pre-workshop preparation. By reflecting upon what matters to them if they think about the topic of the shared moment (workshop), they are forced to explore different angles of the topic and assess which one speaks to them most. That sounds like a perfect way to prime them with a clear personal perspective to kickstart the collaboration.

Getting participants to care about the topic of the co-creation is a key requirement to get them to make deep space for the moment. It increases the potential of the co-creation. It leads to better outcomes.

I use a triangle template that guides participants in their reflections. The template provides questions about the trigger, how it relates to self, and what contextual aspects make it more relevant. Similar to the explanation before in the "PERSONAL EXPERIMENTS" section, I ask them to reflect from three angles:

1. What opportunity do you see in this co-creative moment that catches your attention?
2. Does it resonate with your way of thinking and doing things? Does it stir up strong emotions?
3. Does it resonate with how you want to work and connect with others, or does it impact how you are perceived by others?

I ask them to "hook and harmonize." They have to scan opportunities, find the most compelling one, and find the right depth in articulating the three answers to end up at a triangle that enthuses them to engage.

The task to build their triangle can be introduced by the hook(s) you add into the invitation, like the quote and question in the previous "invitation" example. If you already suggest reasons that move them, they get a headstart to come up with their three angles; their narratives.

Example (continued):

SITUATION You have organized a meeting with a couple of colleagues from other departments who recently completed a project successfully. They had the same challenge your team is currently facing. They will present the full project to your team in this meeting.

INVITATION HOOK
Quote
"Innovation comes from people meeting up in the hallways or calling each other at 10:30 at night with a new idea, or because they realized something that shoots holes in how we've been thinking about a problem. It's ad hoc meetings of six people called by someone who thinks he has figured out the coolest new thing ever and who wants to know what other people think of his idea."

Question
"When did a novel solution ever come from the same thinking in your work?"
A *participant's triangle*

TRIGGER "This could give me a glimpse of how he got to this amazing leftfield approach he used to solve a similar problem."

SELF "All the great ideas I came up with were always inspired by other people, especially outside of the team, even outside of the company. It can be so refreshing to learn from someone from another discipline or industry."

CONTEXT "This will help us to look more often outside for inspiration. It will also make us question our conventional thinking more, not having all the answers. Applying inspiration from outside has made me come across as a very innovative thinker among my peers."

The added hook in the invitation clearly set off the exploration of the triangle. It gave some extra perspective on the value of the gathering and influenced how the participants shaped their narratives to make space.

HOOK INTO A SPIRIT OF COLLECTIVITY

As a facilitator, I often start a workshop by asking everyone to reflect individually on the question, "In what way can this workshop with this topic really matter to you?" The exercise continues with a dialogue with someone else from the team about this question. After the dialogue, I randomly ask people in the group to share if they had the same answer or were surprised by a new perspective. When I feel it can add value, I ask everyone to write their final answer on a Post-it and stick it to the "spirit of collectivity" wall, a canvas prominently positioned in the workshop area. When finished, I introduce this wall as evidence of us being a collective with important stakes in this workshop. Some stakes are the same, and some are different. And I call out some of the shared and surprising answers.

Facilitators consider this a "check-in" or "inclusion" exercise used to get a team in the right frame of mind. Sharing these hooks and the reasoning behind them brings people together in empathy. This sharing increases the pull of the hooks because they have a sense of belonging to a group for whom this topic matters. Sharing a pull increases it.

Such a "check-in" exercise can be the perfect first workshop activity when everyone was tasked before to prepare triangles as pre-work. And this individual pre-work before the workshop can be inspired by the hook(s) already mentioned in your invitation. Sounds like a great group experiment to try out in your next facilitation endeavor.

Dear Diary,

I recently returned from a retreat. It was about finding your purpose. Aaaargh! I don't know. I think I am being overly critical again. The retreat left me more confused than enlightened. I am not sure whether it was the nature of the retreat or just my mind running over. Since things became hectic and pressured, I can't seem to turn it off. Anyway. I struggle with this idea that there is a life path to follow. Do I have a duty, a responsibility? Will I get sick if I'm on the "wrong" path? As life's way of telling me I am born to be or do something else? Will I only find happiness if I figure out the big reason why I am here? What an odd way of thinking. It feels like it is just another way of trying to control life. I want to live as if any moment can matter. Whatever comes around the bend. Even the most challenging moments have a silver lining, I have discovered. And suppose a moment only just provides a different point of view and thereby broadens my horizon. In that case, it is already worth stepping into it without any prejudice and with my full presence. What if we got it all backward by searching for the big overall purpose to understand ourselves better? I think I will understand myself better if I find out why any moment in my life can matter to me again and again, however big, however small. Especially the ones I share with other people. Especially the ones I share with other people who are completely different than me. That sounds to me like a fulfilling way to live. A path to wisdom. Not knowing where it is supposed to be going but enjoying every surprise it brings. I just need to be able to remain open and not have "busyness" get the best of me or unconsciously get stuck in the rigid thinking of a running mind. I should often let go of everything, questioning all my beliefs, ready to replace them with new ones at any given moment. How liberating that would be.

Your Vaganaut

CHAPTER 5.
DEPATTERNING

IT HAD BEEN three years since our last in-person gathering, though occasional video calls had kept us somewhat connected during the pandemic. As we reunited, there was a palpable sense of excitement filled with smiles and warm embraces. We became good friends when working together on a project nearly ten years ago, and our different personalities and expertise created a great synergy.

Frank, the consummate host, had recommended the restaurant, leveraging his deep connections in the hospitality industry. True to form, he ordered a spread of appetizers, his expertise in the culinary arts creating an inviting atmosphere. His stories about the wine and dishes enhanced every bite, transporting us to a familiar ritual of indulgence.

Ben, ever the attentive listener, kicked off the conversation with a genuine inquiry into our lives. His trustworthy presence and kindness invited vulnerability, though he initially deflected the question, preferring to hear our stories first. It became evident that Ben found comfort in offering wisdom to others but remained guarded about his own struggles.

Frank launched into an open account of his work life, finding an eager audience in Ben's wisdom and life experience. Meanwhile, ever the provocateur, Mark bluntly steered our conversation to my wife's gardening experiments, recalling the details with uncanny precision. His spontaneity and wit injected humor and depth, though hinting at a desire for the stability that eluded him.

> *It takes some awareness of your patterns to be able to depattern.*

As we savored the main course, reminiscing about past projects and the joys of collaboration, I took a moment to observe the dynamics of our friendship. Ben's philosophical interpretations, Frank's passionate opinions, and Mark's quirky provocations created a rich combination of charm and personality. Yet, beneath the evolving contexts and topics, I was struck by the familiarity of our roles and patterns, as if we were running the same program, refreshed but unchanged.

Frank's frustrations, Ben's guarded advice, and Mark's humorous deflections echoed our past conversations, a testament to the enduring nature of our friendship. Despite the upheavals in our lives, we fell into the same rhythms, our bonds transcending time and circumstance.

During the dinner, I found myself pausing, struck by a moment of clarity. I shared with my friends that I had become more of an observer than a participant in our conversation. "It's odd, isn't it?" I mused aloud. "We're circling the same topics and emotions as we did years ago." Although my observation amused them, and they acknowledged the recurring patterns, they quickly resumed their discussions as if nothing had been pointed out, and the evening unfolded predictably.

Despite this, there was a palpable commitment to the moment among us. Ben eventually opened up about some complexities in his work life, seeking our insights. Frank vented about his consulting challenges, while Mark discussed his current relationship, looking for support. Having been isolated in formal, predominantly online work environments, I was simply savoring the camaraderie. One of the remarkable aspects of our gatherings was our undivided attention to one another – an increasingly rare quality. Still, it felt like we didn't make a lot of space. Despite our switches and hooks, there wasn't a lot of space for any novelty, anything surprising, or any magical insights.

The evening lacked novelty. While deeply engaging, our conversations felt too familiar, almost as if we were replaying well-worn scripts. Although we were fully present, our dialogue seemed confined within predefined patterns, leaving little room for unexpected insights. Even Mark's sharp wit, which occasionally jolted us, couldn't fully disrupt the comfortable predictability of our interaction.

You might have experienced similar situations during family dinners or reunions with long-time friends. Despite personal growth and change, these interactions can sometimes resurrect an outdated version of ourselves – one that we might have moved beyond. Reflecting on these moments often reveals a dissonance between our current self and the persona that was unwittingly revived. When we run our programs and play out our patterns, we do not keep the space open. It is filled with often unconscious behavior, repeating the known, the familiar. To truly elevate our interactions from mere collaboration to genuine co-creation, we have **to depattern ourselves in order to make space**.

This might be the most difficult tenet of the five. It takes some awareness of your patterns to be able to depattern. You have to become more of an observer of self versus identifying with self. Self, being the person you think you are or should be. It is a mind-bender to observe yourself while being yourself.

Mastering this tenet can be challenging in practice. Yet, it is crucial to understand why meetings, brainstorming sessions, and family gatherings often yield predictable outcomes and evoke familiar feelings. The difficulty in achieving unconventional results often stems from the entrenched dynamics within teams – those who have spent years in the same roles, within the same company culture, or among similar types of people. In such environments, it becomes impossible to make space for creation, dominated instead by routine collaboration.

BRAINY PATTERNS

Our brain is the most energy-consuming part of our body. Lisa Feldman Barrett, a neuroscientist and psychologist, explains in her book *How Emotions Are Made: The Secret Life of the Brain* that our brains are primarily built for energy efficiency through a predictive coding mechanism. According to her theory, the brain's main function is to predict and anticipate incoming sensory inputs based on past experiences and internal world models. By making efficient predictions, the brain conserves energy by minimizing the need to constantly process sensory information. This energy-efficient, predictive coding system allows the brain to prioritize relevant information and respond quickly to changes in the environment while conserving resources. It means our past experiences and expectations influence our interpretation of events and interactions with others.

According to Lisa Feldman Barrett, our brain's coding mechanisms significantly influence our behavior through several pathways. Our actions are often shaped by patterns formed from past experiences, cultural norms, social expectations, and personal beliefs. Behaviors reinforced by positive outcomes tend to be

The most transformative journey one can undertake is the quest for personal growth through self-awareness, specifically by recognizing and understanding your intrinsic patterns.

repeated, becoming automatic and ingrained over time. Additionally, we frequently model our behavior on that of others, especially those seen as role models or authority figures, including influences from family, peers, and media. Our brain's tendency to be efficient, relying on shortcuts and heuristics, can lead to persistent, yet sometimes irrational, patterns known as cognitive biases.

Our thoughts and behaviors are deeply patterned. The brain continuously seeks out and recognizes patterns, shaping our thinking and, consequently, our behaviors.

The most transformative journey one can undertake is the quest for personal growth through self-awareness, specifically by recognizing and understanding our intrinsic patterns.

LET THE GENIUS OUT OF THE BOTTLE

Depatterning, recognizing, and letting go of our existing patterns starts with becoming conscious of them. It means climbing outside the bottle to read the label. You become an observer of your own thoughts, feelings, and behavior.

The biggest obstacle I face in self-observation is my own state of being. When overwhelmed by stress, tension, anger, or frustration, it becomes nearly impossible to observe myself without attaching to my emotions. There is no chance to step back and objectively assess both the situation and my reactions – physically and mentally. This is often referred to as "being too much in your head and not in your heart."

> *A relaxed state is crucial to become aware of your patterns.*

Our culture is rich with folklore and symbolism about the dangers of being in our heads too much. Yet, ironically, we now live in an era of unprecedented distraction, where we are more caught up in our heads than ever before. While I cannot recall any past lives to confirm this, it seems likely that our current age is uniquely characterized by this challenge.

THE SWORD OF DAMOCLES: Damocles is granted the opportunity to sit on the king's throne. However, above his head hangs a sword suspended by a single hair, symbolizing the constant fear and anxiety accompanying positions of power and privilege. It is a metaphor for the burden of excessive mental worry and insecurity.

THE HYDRA: The multi-headed serpent-like creature that grows two heads for each one that is cut off. Hercules has to cauterize each neck stump to prevent new heads from growing. Hydra symbolizes the endless proliferation of distracting or negative thoughts and the need to confront and overcome them.

THE HEADLESS HORSEMAN: A ghostly figure riding through the night without a head, carrying a jack-o'-lantern or skull in his hand. This story represents the liberation from excessive mental attachment and identification with the ego, suggesting that true freedom comes from transcending the limitations of the mind.

THE TWO WOLVES: A Native American Cherokee legend of a grandfather teaching his grandson about life. He explains that there are two wolves battling inside each person: one representing negativity, fear, and anger, and the other representing positivity, love, and peace. The one that wins is the one you feed.

MONKEY MIND: This concept, rooted in Buddhist philosophy, refers to the restless, unsettled nature of the mind, represented by a monkey jumping from branch to branch. The idea is to quiet the "monkey mind" to achieve greater mental clarity and peace.
Our mental state often becomes the most significant barrier to calming the mind. When our thoughts fully capture our attention – particularly when they are intensified by emotions – we start to identify with this mental chatter. Believing every thought as truth, we metaphorically "jump into the bottle," losing the ability to read the label. This cycle of believing our thoughts fuels our emotions, leading us to embody these thoughts and adopt a state of anxiety, restlessness, and concern. We make ourselves as small as our thoughts, letting our thoughts define us.

Organizations characterized by high pressure and stress often develop a culture rooted in unconscious behavioral patterns. When a group collectively experiences a stress-driven culture, it fosters shared unconscious behaviors, making little space for co-creation. Instead, employees repeatedly do what they believe is expected, adhering to the familiar. To break free from these patterns, it is not enough to merely avoid them; rather, it requires a conscious effort to recognize and understand them.

A relaxed state is crucial to become aware of your own patterns and those of others. Stress typically heightens your identification with your thoughts, making it difficult to recognize these patterns. Conversely, a relaxed state facilitates the ability to observe your behaviors more objectively. Meditation practitioners often train to enter this relaxed state more readily, disengaging from their thoughts. Monitoring and managing your state is essential, especially if you are not feeling relaxed. Shifting from stress to relaxation is crucial for getting out of the bottle and observing your patterns. This transition may be challenging for those frequently experiencing anxiety, but it becomes easier with practice. As you habitually move into an observer's mindset, your brain adapts, recognizing and enabling this shift more swiftly. This process essentially reprograms your brain's efficiency mechanism, making each subsequent transition smoother.

Simple practices to go from an anxious to a relaxed state so you can become an observer of your thoughts, feelings, and behaviors are explained in the PERSONAL EXPERIMENT? section later in this chapter.

Managing your state removes the obstacle to letting your genius out of the bottle. You become aware of your patterns. Increasing such awareness makes space for new thinking, feeling, or doing. You are making space for the unknown.

UNLIMITED EXPLORATION OUTSIDE THE BOTTLE
Becoming aware of your tendencies is how we start depatterning for co-creation. But it needs to happen with acceptance and compassion. Judging your tendencies may trigger a stress response, making it hard to remain an observer. It is tricky. The best way to remember why it is important to stay calm and not judge your patterns when you become aware of them is to understand the benefits of sustaining a relaxed state. What are the benefits of calming down when we get stressed?

Inducing a parasympathetic response in our autonomic nervous systems, or simply calming down, activates our vagal nerve, which triggers the release of acetylcholine. The effect of this release helps with depatterning our ways of thinking:

- It supports the brain's ability to reorganize and form new connections, called neuroplasticity.
- It allows for sustained focus while enabling flexible thinking and idea generation.

- It aids in accessing and combining past experiences and knowledge to generate novel ideas and solutions.
- It promotes a state of relaxed alertness conducive to creative thinking.
- It facilitates the integration of information from diverse brain regions for creative insights and problem-solving.

In other words, being at peace with your patterns allows you to let go of them.

In this ideal calm state, there are three approaches you can practice to spark depatterning. Three approaches to make space *during* the moment, while the switch and the hook happen *before* the moment. These three approaches to depatterning prevent filling the space with your unconscious patterns. Instead, they make space for the unknown, which is the crux of creation.

When in a calm state, you can depattern by:

1. using variety and diversity
2. using silence
3. looking for blind spots.

These approaches make space for the unknown. Let me explain the theory behind them before we move into practices for experimentation.

1. Our differences are our strength

At the beginning of my career, when I was working in marketing for a large organization, I collaborated with a marketing consultant who specialized in helping organizations become more customer-centric. A professor in marketing who wrote a couple of books on customer centricity and provided keynotes and workshops to rethink the delivery of services from the perspective of customers or consumers. I was captivated by one of the books and invited him to lead a workshop with a group of my colleagues. His workshop started with an inspiring presentation followed by some exercises to help us create our action plan. When he presented and gave instructions, it made so much sense. Whichever way he explained it, it resonated with everyone. It was common sense, but for some reason, it hadn't naturally occurred to our minds before. When he laid it out for us, we all nodded in agreement as if someone had turned on a light.

> *As people interact, their thought fields can influence one another.*

When any of us tried to reproduce the explanations and concepts afterward, at a later moment, to other people, the stories that came out weren't as coherent as his. It would be some bits and pieces with improvisation and personal interpretation to fill in the gaps, like telling a joke at a cocktail party, which you just heard for the first time a couple of days before, and struggling to properly deliver the punchline.

A couple of weeks after the workshop, we presented our outcomes to management, but I found myself unable to reproduce the stories with the same compelling impact as when originally delivered by the professor – an experience I've encountered numerous times from both speaker and listener perspectives. As a trainer and speaker, I've had people quote me verbatim yet hear my words reshaped into different versions, revealing how personal interpretations can lack the essence of the intended message. Conversely, as an audience member, I've frequently attempted to retell a captivating narrative learned from an expert, only to fail in conveying that gripping spirit.

VARIETY IN MINDS
In energy psychology, the concept of thought fields explains this phenomenon of perceiving concepts more clearly in the presence of an expert. Thoughts and emotions are believed to generate energetic patterns or fields around individuals. As people interact, their thought fields can influence one another. This suggests that beyond simply offering new perspectives during a conversation, the mere presence of individuals with diverse thought fields can trigger us to understand and perceive things differently. This diversity of thought fields helps us depattern or break free from habitual thinking due to the interference between these varied energetic fields. Just as one can experience a sudden clarity when a scientist explains their research in person, it becomes more challenging to maintain that same level of understanding later, without their presence. This highlights the power of diversity in presence, where the convergence of varied thought fields can enhance our comprehension and perception.

According to the same theory of thought fields, when a group of individuals interact repeatedly over multiple occasions, collective thought fields within that group can emerge. These collective thought fields possess shared beliefs and drive collective behavior, shaping the group's culture, as described earlier in this chapter. Groups, communities, or even larger populations can develop these collective thought fields that hold and perpetuate common beliefs and patterns of behavior.

Although the existence of thought fields is still a theoretical concept and an area of ongoing scientific exploration and debate, it helps to imagine the value of bringing a variety of different people to a moment. People from different teams, different departments, different backgrounds, different organizations, people with different thinking and behavioral patterns, and people from different cultures with different patterns. Their participation can help break our individual patterns and team patterns.

VARIETY IN ACTIVITIES

Bringing in different minds, like adding a different way of thinking to the mix, is one way to depattern. Another way of increasing variety to depattern is to introduce different behaviors during an interaction.

Introducing changes to the rules of an interaction can help individuals disengage from the self-images and identities they unconsciously uphold. Many people inadvertently adopt roles and behavioral patterns nurtured by how they perceive their worth and importance within the organizational culture. However, disrupting the typical norms and turning the established way of doing things upside down in the micro-environment of a shared moment can depattern the participants' habitual thinking and behavior. Individuals are liberated from their accustomed roles and the associated social constructs as the familiar dynamics are upended.

Disruptions introduced must be significant enough to effectively break ingrained patterns. A common misconception is that simply introducing creative furniture or inspiring wall decor will suffice in breaking people's established patterns. It does not. It just gives the existing patterns a different flavor. To break patterns, you have to first identify some patterns to break. For instance, if the organizational culture typically demands obedient and respectful behavior toward superiors, an interesting approach could be to create the opposite hierarchical setting by assigning new titles to everyone.

Language often serves as a perfect reflection of a particular culture. The terminology, the formal or informal modes of address, and even the expressions commonly used by everyone, such as "moving the needle," "let's make it measurable with KPIs," what's in our backlog," "let's get everyone on the same page," are expressions of that culture. Using specific terminology, expressions, and acronyms is often an important tool for individuals to play their roles within cultural norms. One effective way to disrupt these ingrained patterns is by stripping down the familiar language and introducing a new one. For example, a rule that prohibits using acronyms, expressions, or complex terminology during the shared experience could be established. Whenever someone inadvertently uses such language, they would be required to rephrase or explain their statement. Another approach could involve implementing a rule that every story told must be conveyed using language as if speaking to a friend at a garden party.

You can also break your personal patterns when becoming aware of them. Instead of introducing new rules to adopt by a group, introduce variety yourself in how you think or engage with others. If you've recognized that you often play the devil's advocate in most work conversations, you can address your risk aversion by consciously deciding to seek out valuable, bold, and risky initiatives. Rather than playing it safe and structured, you can become the person who dares to explore and embrace uncertainty. The beauty of observing your own patterns lies in the revelation of countless possibilities to disrupt and break free of your ingrained habits.

Silence can also be an incredibly powerful way to introduce variety if you tend to have all the answers all the time and always immediately express whatever comes to mind without filters or delay.

2. *The power of silence*

My wife and I participated in a weekend-long plant medicine ceremony led by an experienced shaman called the "Laughing Shaman." When we left for the weekend, we both felt some level of anxiety about the unknown. We had no idea what to expect from such a deep dive into ourselves. Would any unexpected layers from our subconscious be revealed? Would that feel liberating or plain scary?

The experience left me with a renewed and profound understanding of the power of silence. Throughout the weekend, the shaman's facilitation skills were put to the test, especially when our group of diverse personalities, after being transported to the deepest layers of our subconscious, found ourselves fragile and confused. It was in those vulnerable moments, as we shared our experiences, personal stories, and even our greatest fears and challenges in life with one another, that the shaman's true facilitation prowess came into play.

As the weekend progressed, the shaman's effective use of silence took on a profound role in holding the space and guiding us through trauma despite being complete strangers at the outset. At first, the moments of silence seemed to serve the obvious purpose of allowing everyone an opportunity to speak. However, as we delved deeper into sharing and forging connections, vulnerability peaked, and the stories became overwhelmingly raw. People revealed their deepest hurts and life's most formidable obstacles. It was then that the shaman's wielding of silence developed a whole new meaning for me.

It was like I suddenly understood – for the first time – what the sound of silence truly is. It is the sound of creation.

As these profound moments unfolded, I paid close attention to the effect that the invoked silence had on their depth and intensity. Whenever a moment of silence occurred naturally or by invitation, I tried to be very conscious of what the silence did for us. Through this deliberate awareness, I captured three distinct perspectives on the power of silence and its ability to disrupt ingrained patterns, or in other words, what I've come to call depatterning: the channel, the shift, and the cleanse.

It was like I suddenly understood – for the first time – what the sound of silence truly is. It is the sound of creation.

THE CHANNEL

We connect through the act of listening and sharing stories, driven by a deep-seated social urge to forge and reinforce bonds. This inherent social instinct binds us through storytelling, immersing us deeply in a narrative, wrapped up in the thoughts and emotions it evokes. It can fill the entire shared space. Our feelings triggered by a story can overtake us and put us in a state. They can become sticky.

Silence can serve as a tool to temper the deluge of our thoughts and our impulse to respond, allowing us to be fully present while someone shares their story. During our sharing moments after the ceremonies, our shaman made sure that each person could fully tell their story and share their thoughts before others could reply. This practice gave listeners a moment to pause, absorbing the narrative deeply before crafting their responses. It also ensured that the storyteller could express themselves uninterrupted, preventing their train of thought from being prematurely disrupted. This way of holding the space for each speaker helps prevent premature interactions.

Nevertheless, when a story or opinion is fully shared and other people start responding, the conversation that follows fills the space. When thoughts and emotions become "sticky," repeating what has already been expressed in different words by various individuals no longer provides new insights. However, during our weekend, ample silence punctuated the sharing of thoughts.

By intentionally providing moments of silence, you allow for the release of a flow of thoughts, creating space for new ones to emerge organically without forcing associations with previous ideas. Silence can also be a conscious choice to make space for others instead of immediately sharing the thoughts occupying your mind. By refraining from voicing those thoughts, even if they seem valuable, you cultivate greater awareness of your own thinking patterns. This act of not expressing your thoughts is a literal practice of letting go, detaching yourself from those mental patterns – an act of depatterning. Not only are you making space for others, but you are actively making space for new thinking within yourself. When you bring together a diversity of minds and embrace silence, you make space for the other minds to share, allowing their fresh perspectives to help depattern you from your established knowns.

Those moments of silence you deliberately install are mini-moments of space that allow for the unknown to arise. Whether it comes from a different type of mind or a non-local field of "who knows what," it will likely be more qualitative than your programmed thinking. It is a form of

> *Those moments of silence you deliberately install are mini-moments of space that allow for the unknown to arise.*

refueling, channeling new extra thoughts to mix into the sharing, reducing the repetition of what has already been said.

Making space with silence usually doesn't happen this way during work meetings and workshops. Instead, people often force their opinions into the shared space, sometimes even trying to crowd out other people's opinions to control the conversation.

THE SHIFT

When we share our own opinion or story or respond to someone's opinion, it often comes from a place of identifying with something. It may mean we express ourselves from the perspective of our professional role, a title we have been given, or a place of suffering we feel as victims of injustice or trauma. It can turn sharing moments into battles of the ego, whether or not we mean it to.

During our weekend of sharing the darkest of emotions, the shaman elegantly guided us into fully accepting and being present with those emotions and situations. When revealing our stories, objectivity was inherently absent, for these were our lives, our pain – we were the stories we told ourselves. By embodying these stories, we lacked the higher perspective to view them objectively. Resisting or falling into victimhood reinforced our identification with the stories, fostering blind spots. However, by accepting them with full presence, our perspective suddenly shifted. To be truly objective, we cannot be the very object we're contemplating. As the adage goes, "You cannot read the label from inside the bottle."

After sharing one's thoughts, installing a deliberate moment of silence can facilitate detachment from those very ideas. This silence serves to shift one's perspective from being subjective and enmeshed within a fixed way of thinking about a situation toward a more objective stance. Space is needed for this continuous subject-object shift – a space that can be created through the intentional invocation of silence, which we refer to as "the shift."

Space is needed for this continuous subject-object shift

THE CLEANSE

To allow for a fresh perspective or to introduce a new topic, the space needs to be cleared, opening participants' minds. This is what I call "the cleanse."

Akin to cleansing one's palette while enjoying a magnificent meal, having been immersed in the flavors of a delicious starter, you now prepare to taste a completely different main course.

Our shaman patiently waited in silence as each sharing moment came to an end. Somehow intuitively, we all felt when everything had been said, ready for someone else's story to be shared. I was amazed by how intuitively we, as a group, could transition from one topic to another, bridged by a cleansing moment of silence. An important collective letting go of one topic to make space for the next. That cleansing silence was a vital moment of closure for everyone, helping us all become present again to continue sharing together.

I wish such intuitive transitions from topic to topic occurred during meetings and workshops. Usually, people do not instinctively create space to end one topic and allow for a new one. Instead, they talk over others, randomly interjecting thoughts without first actively listening to what has been previously shared.

The power of silence can be applied in myriad ways. From the perspective of making space for co-creation, these three approaches to silence – the channel, the shift, and the cleanse – can help depattern ingrained habits. Yet, we have become unaccustomed to silence in our lives. Noise pollution has increased dramatically in recent years, and we have filled our lives with distractions, cluttering the space. Silence has become uncomfortable for many. It also amplifies our "Monkey Mind," generating feelings of anxiety, like "there is still so much to do, and there shouldn't be any time for silence." We need to rekindle our bond with silence, one of the most powerful ways to become aware of and break free from our patterns.

3. Blind spots are where the monsters hide

Depatterning is making space for the unknown, but the unknown can provoke fear – a lack of control, uncertainty, and discomfort that shakes the foundations of our beliefs. There might be monsters hiding in the unknown. The known feels safe and requires less mental energy to process. Our brains are biased toward the familiar, as it helps us make sense of the world. By deliberately seeking out blind spots, we go against this bias that causes us to think and behave in patterns. We can depattern our thinking and behavior by directing our attention toward what we don't know.

But looking for blind spots can feel uncomfortable, an unhinging thing to do. It can feel counterintuitive. This discomfort stems from our ego – perhaps the best starting point when seeking out blind spots.

Our ego is an amazing psychological mechanism that evolved to help us navigate our environment and ensure our survival. It operates based on deeply ingrained survival instincts designed to protect us from perceived threats or dangers. Our ego is concerned with self-preservation, protection, and fulfilling our basic needs. We need to survive physically, but our identity also needs to thrive – our status in relation to others and our sense of security. While we should celebrate our ego for keeping us alive and relevant, it is also the most important cause of our blind spots and a key driver of our thinking and behavior patterns.

A lack of empathy, short-sightedness beyond our expertise, ignorance of stories with no immediate "value," lack of motivation for distant events, evading the needs of new hires, and overlooking the possibility of being wrong despite strong opinions – these are all results of ego-driven patterns.

I'm not suggesting that every blind spot stems from the limitations of the ego. Rather, I propose that the most effective way to depattern is by transcending ego-driven patterns. I would also never suggest that the ego is bad or should be avoided. On the contrary, our ego is an amazing mechanism that should be embraced and appreciated. But to depattern, you need to be aware of your ego-driven patterns rather than being blinded by them.

These are three typical characteristics of ego-driven patterns of thinking and behavior:

> *This discomfort stems from our ego – perhaps the best starting point when seeking out blind spots.*

Me, Myself, and I Syndrome: Refers to our tendency to prioritize our needs and desires above others. Our focus is on personal gain, recognition, or validation, sometimes at the expense of others' well-being or the greater good.

Ego Forcefield: Describes the reactive defensiveness when our self-image or identity is challenged. Typically, justifying our actions or beliefs and avoiding criticism or feedback that contradicts our self-perception.

Stuck-in-the-Mud Mindset: Our inflexibility and unwillingness to change. Holding on to familiar beliefs, habits, or ways of thinking, even in the face of evidence or feedback suggesting that change is necessary or beneficial. Thus, looking for personal gain, defending our identity, and holding on to certainty are three simple yet universal characteristics to search for to deliberately uncover our blind spots. By frequently checking for these characteristics, you can develop a sixth sense for noticing when your ego is creeping up on you. Whenever you experience strong emotions or feel your body sending signals in your stomach or gut, it's an opportune moment to cross-check with these three aspects to identify potential blind spots. Sensations in your stomach or gut area are part of the body's natural reaction to consciously or unconsciously perceived threats; these can be threats to the ego.

Let's experiment with depatterning, personally and in a group.

DEPATTERNING
Experiments

PERSONAL EXPERIMENT

The aim of this practice is to make space for the unknown. Our patterns of thinking and behavior keep us trapped in the known. Even if we have made deep space for connection by "switching" and "hooking," if we fill up the space with our unconscious patterns, there will still be little space left for co-creation.

MY PERSONAL PRACTICE
Depatterning is one of the key practices in my own work, and I strongly believe it is "the" path toward my self-growth, more important than any other growth practice I have adopted over the years. Depatterning is the essence of making space and the most difficult tenet to apply as it directly confronts your sense of self.

I keep my practices in depatterning lighthearted and fun because there is a risk of causing internal conflict.

Managing my state has become second nature. Separate from any depatterning practices, I think everyone should consider learning how to easily return from a stressed state. Training yourself to trigger your parasympathetic response whenever you get stressed improves life quality, wiring your brain and increasing your vagal tone in the process.

I have weekly routines of exercise, breathwork, quiet introspection, and heat and cold exposure. These practices maintain a high vagal tone and the ability to easily shift to a calm state. To ensure you find something sustainable for years, include activities you truly enjoy in your routine and evolve them if the enjoyment fades. The worst thing you can do is try to adopt activities like meditation, breathwork, or yoga just because you read about them or someone told you to. Your routines need to excite you, and you need to long for them. It could be dance, weekly karaoke, reading novels, or taking hot baths, as long as they help you wind down into a relaxed state, and you can build a frequent routine around them. Repetitively triggering a parasympathetic response will make it easier over time.

Assuming I am in a calm state, I depattern with variety, silence, and blind spots in a few intuitive ways.

Whenever I get clear about my intention during the switch and shape my hook from the angle of self and in relation to others, there is always an element of seeking variety. I see every shared moment as an opportunity for co-creation. Switching and getting hooked into the moment already gets me thinking about what can be leveraged to gain new insights and arrive at interesting outcomes. I long for depatterning and get excited if I see a chance for synergy and serendipity leading to novelty. This is almost always part of my hook and influences my intent.

When I start engaging, my mantra is "hold the space to reveal the hidden treasures." Silence is my friend, the sound of creation. I use it consciously to avoid getting trapped in my own thoughts and to make space for the surprises others can bring. I consciously hold back on sharing my ideas to make space for others and observe all the tiny details happening in the shared space. When I notice patterns in others, I play on them to get interesting content out. If I see someone becoming emotional about making their point, overanalyzing, or disagreeing all the time, I leverage the pattern to mine their mind. These habits from years of facilitating workshops come in handy to make space for the unknowns.

Some meetings and workshops pose a bigger risk for my ego-driven patterns than others. When the topic potentially threatens self-images I am aware of, like being a good facilitator or a valuable consultant, I am more on guard and ask myself three ego-related questions more often to avoid being blinded. When the topic feels less sensitive, I don't ask the three questions as much.

Not taking yourself too seriously and being on guard whenever you become emotional or strong-headed about something, combined with a love for silence and nothingness, can turn all your collaborations into co-creations.

Silence is a blank canvas, ready to become a masterpiece.

Depatterning requires you to be in a "relax and digest" state as opposed to a tense "fight or flight" state. Starting from the right state, these personal practices use variety, silence, and blind spots to elevate your collaboration to co-creation, achieving better outcomes from your meetings and workshops.

HOW TO MANAGE YOUR STATE TO ALLOW FOR DEPATTERNING

A change of state can facilitate the depatterning of our thinking by loosening our grip on deeply held beliefs. When we are not under pressure, it becomes easier to observe our patterns rather than be consumed by them. This phenomenon helps explain why great ideas often materialize on a napkin while enjoying a cold beer or a glass of wine. There is even a theory suggesting that psychedelics played a role in humanity's adaptation for survival due to their "depatterning factor," enabling populations to break free from old patterns and adopt radically innovative perceptions and behaviors. In the "Stoned Ape Theory," Terence McKenna proposes that the ingestion of psychedelics could have led to cognitive enhancements that facilitated the development of language and other complex cognitive processes, ultimately contributing to the rapid evolution of the human brain and culture.

Luckily, it is not necessary to take substances to get into a state that allows for new insights, for the unknown.

The rest and digest state is the opposite of the fight or flight state. They can't exist at the same time, but the change from one to the other can happen rapidly. In particular, the shift from the (calm) rest and digest state toward the (tense) flight or fight state can happen in an instant for some people. Some of us spend most of our time during the day in a state of tension. Returning to a calm state from a tense state can be much harder than losing your cool.

These states aren't binary but exist on a spectrum. There are multiple versions of calm, ranging from an imaginative, playful state to daydreaming, a meditative state, and deep sleep. Similarly, there are various states of not being calm and relaxed, spanning from alertness, vigilance, anxiety, stress, and fear to obsession. In the middle lies a balanced state called "relaxed focus." This spectrum of states has "deep rest" on one end and "highly threatened" on the other.

During our working day, we might alternate between a state of imagination and a state of vigilance. Some individuals experience more tension and spend their working day fluctuating between alertness, vigilance, and anxiety, potentially peaking at times into stress. I interpret this spectrum as having a gravitational pull toward each end from a certain tipping point on either side. This means that once you are in a meditative state, you can easily slip into a sleeping state. Conversely, once you are in an anxious state, you can readily move into a stressed or even threatened state.

The way you move across this spectrum depends on the way your brain is programmed. The wiring of your brain is shaped by your past experiences, coming from thinking, doing, and feeling cycles. Your thinking leads to your doing, and experiencing your doing generates emotions that shape your thinking and create memories, which again impact your doing. If you spend a lot of time in stressful situations, your brain is wired to easily get stressed. If you grew up in an ashram and learned to turn inwards to achieve a peaceful state from a young age often, your brain is wired to find peace in all circumstances.

While it may seem like these are mental states, they are more closely tied to bodily states. You cannot simply think yourself into stress; rather, it is an autonomic response in your nervous system, specifically the sympathetic response, which is triggered by association. When something is perceived as threatening due to past memories, the stress response occurs in the blink of an eye. You don't consciously relive all the memories to decide whether you will feel stressed. Instead, it is an autonomic response that induces a bodily state caused by the release of stress hormones into your bloodstream, triggered in the center of your brain.

It is equally challenging to think your way into calmness when stressed. This is also an autonomic response in your nervous system, known as the parasympathetic response, in which your longest brain nerve, the vagus nerve, plays a crucial role. We have a vagal tone that can be measured, for example, by measuring heart rate variability to indicate the activity level of our vagus nerve. This activity level is associated with our ability to regulate our stress response and promote relaxation. In other words, some individuals can more easily transition from a stressed to a calm state than others. These individuals have a higher vagal tone.

In both calm and tense states, these are bodily conditions that influence our thinking and behavior. A tense bodily state is a state of survival, meaning it is not conducive to being imaginative. Evolution has developed this mechanism to deal with threats by fighting or fleeing. To act quickly, we act from what we know, not from what we can imagine. A tense state can also be seen as an ego state with tunnel vision focused solely on self-preservation. You cannot think your way out of tunnel vision, as your thinking is influenced by your bodily state. To broaden your thinking again, you have to feel your way out of this state by focusing on relaxing your body.

To transition from a tense state to a calm one and loosen your grip on what you know, you must work on your body by activating your vagus nerve to trigger a parasympathetic response. A tense state provides an ego perspective focused on self-preservation and stimulates patterned thinking and behavior. In contrast, a calm state promotes imagination, is less fixated on identity, and makes space for the unknown, making it a prerequisite for depatterning.

Great news! The practices of switching, finding your hook, and harmonizing have likely already helped you relax into the shared moment. These practices trigger a parasympathetic response by removing friction toward the upcoming moment and encouraging emotional investment in the moment. In particular, gratitude for a shared moment will trigger a parasympathetic response that promotes feelings of contentment and well-being. However, this is not a certainty. If you have a low vagal tone and lead a stressful life, you might still find yourself on the spectrum of vigilance or even anxiety. While you may have created some space, there's a chance you will fill it with your unconscious thinking and behavioral patterns. As a part of these patterns, you might also be easily triggered up the spectrum toward stress, making you even less aware of your conditioned responses. To help you come down from a stressed bodily state and practice this shift frequently so that your brain becomes wired for it, let's explore some simple techniques you can use to achieve calmness before and during your shared moment.

BEFORE YOUR SHARED MOMENT OR DURING A BREAK
Humming or even a little bit of singing as you walk toward the restroom, the parking lot, or the meeting location. Vibration in your throat stimulates the vagus nerve, and apparently, we can't think when we are humming.

Gargling some water in the restroom. It has the same effect and the same reason as humming or singing.

Neck stretches when you find a moment to yourself. You can design your own routine that works best for you. This releases tension and stimulates the vagus nerve.
Cold water splash. Splashing your face with cold water activates the parasympathetic response. Cold exposure, in general, activates your vagus nerve.

Soothing music. While driving to your meeting or workshop, or in between, when having a break, listen to calming music. Loud, fast-paced rhythms, aggressive instrumentation, and aggressive or emotionally charged lyrics obviously won't have the calming effect needed to help you become an observer of your patterns. On the contrary, it will likely surface your patterns.

Chewing mindfully. If you are having a snack before a meeting or during a break, chewing slowly and bringing your attention to enjoying your food will trigger the calm, rest and digest, state. Although not scientifically proven to work for everyone, chewing gum can also have a similar calming effect. It can improve mood and lower cortisol levels.

Connect. Talking to someone you hold dear can trigger your calm state. A quick phone call to your partner, kid, or any other family or friends will help greatly if the conversation is friendly, fun, or loving. Drop by your befriended colleague's desk for a chat or joke around at the coffee machine. Friendly social interaction activates the vagus nerve and promotes relaxation and emotional regulation.

DURING A SHARED MOMENT

Slow breathing. Notice the pace of your breathing and, if possible, extend it to a four-second in-breath and a four-second out-breath. Now and then, extend your exhale a bit more, especially when bringing your attention back to the moment or transitioning to the next topic. The act of exhaling stimulates the vagus nerve.

Laughter. Laughter stimulates the vagus nerve and triggers a parasympathetic response. Introduce some lighthearted moments in your conversation with anecdotes and friendly jokes.

Positive emotional interaction. Besides jokes, any type of interaction that fosters connection will activate the vagus nerve. Acknowledgments, compliments, and appreciation will trigger a parasympathetic response on both sides. Use your own style; this only works when it is genuine.

Eye contact. Eye contact increases parasympathetic activity and stimulates the vagus nerve. It generates feelings of trust between people, if not culturally conditioned for a different effect.

Tone of voice. By speaking with a calm and relaxing voice, avoiding high-pitched and fast-paced talking, the soothing sound and the vibrations in your throat will stimulate your vagus nerve. It will also have a calming effect on others.

Active listening. Genuine interest in what someone else is saying, asking questions out of curiosity, paraphrasing, and expressing compassion foster connection and thereby stimulate everyone's vagus nerve. Nurturing a sense of belonging will trigger a relaxed state.

A critical mind is filled with patterned thinking, while a relaxed mind makes space. When applying critical thinking, which can trigger sympathetic and defensive responses within the group, ensure that you maintain your relaxed state and remain an observer who can easily let go of beliefs. A relaxed and digest state for depatterning doesn't mean you have to agree with everyone or force yourself into positive emotions. Instead, it means you manage your state by coming back down when you feel yourself moving up the stress spectrum. By doing so, you avoid identifying with any opinions and instead keep the space open, again and again, for the unknown.

Compassion is by far the most powerful emotion to guide you down the spectrum toward a relaxed state, even toward a meditative state. The emotion of compassion is the ultimate catalyst for achieving a state of well-being and relaxation.

HOW TO DEPATTERN USING VARIETY

As a personal experiment, you can depattern using variety in two different ways. If you are aware of some of your typical thinking and behavioral patterns, you can try to counter them by deliberately doing the opposite. If you are not aware of typical patterns or prefer to take a different approach, you can also "mine the minds" present in the shared moment.

COUNTER YOUR PATTERNS

The following examples are based on potential patterns you may exhibit. The first step is to identify some key patterns that often recur – habits you have observed in yourself. The second step is to select the one you will consciously counter during the shared moment. If it consumes all your attention, it won't effectively contribute to achieving a good level of co-creation. Instead, it should be something you keep in the back of your mind, and whenever the opportunity arises, you choose to act differently than your usual behavior.

PATTERN: You deviate into personal anecdotes and engage in conversation solely from your single-minded perspective.
COUNTERACT: *Ask others to share their anecdotes. Frequently consider the potential perspectives of stakeholders who aren't present.*

PATTERN: When people disagree with you, you get caught up in spending too much time and energy reinforcing your points, proving how you are right.
COUNTERACT: *Don't give more than one argumentation. If no one else backs you up and your argumentation doesn't stick, immediately surrender and continue listening to the other's perspectives.*

PATTERN: You interrupt people because you feel you have something more valuable to say that should immediately get everyone's attention.
COUNTERACT: *Only say something when it feels like everyone has finished talking. You are never the first one to take up the space.*

PATTERN: You tend to hijack one person from the group to get your point across and be recognized for your opinion.
COUNTERACT: *Pay attention to ensure that only one conversation is happening at a time. Whenever people start a side conversation, you invite them to share with the entire group.*

PATTERN: You turn everything into a joke, taking the seriousness out of the conversation because you enjoy the attention whenever you can disrupt the tension that arises as others make their points.
COUNTERACT: *Ask people to share their feelings and motivations whenever they share something serious. Pay extra attention to ensuring there is a platform for people to express their emotions. Strive to deepen the conversation at all times.*

PATTERN: You keep asking questions but never state an opinion or take a stand on anything because you are not confident enough about any point of view you have, and you prefer to avoid confrontation.
COUNTERACT: *Turn the points people make into statements for the group to reflect on and evaluate their validity. For example, "So, would it be fair to say … (statement)…?" You don't have to defend your statements; the group evaluates them based on relevance. Take on the role of solidifying conclusions within the group by suggesting statements.*

PATTERN: You get overly excited when making your point, crowding everyone else out of the conversation and filling up the entire space, which overwhelms others. They might even log off during your explanations.
COUNTERACT: *Each time you want to introduce a new idea or concept, announce that you will try to do it concisely, asking for everyone's help to add elements or help shape it. Then, try to tell a stripped-down*

version for the others to enrich. Let it go if it is not as enriched as you think it could be.

PATTERN: You tend to "talk to think," which results in long, incoherent explanations that are hard to follow. Your messages are often not picked up by others.
COUNTERACT: Aim to share only fully formed concepts. If an idea is still a hunch and very rough, don't share it. Instead, write it down to let it take further shape, with the confidence that there will be a suitable time to share it fully later.

PATTERN: You prefer hands-on, structured conversation with facts and actionability. You tend to think in frameworks and to-dos. Your mantra is, "Let's not reinvent the wheel here."
COUNTERACT: Allow others to provide structure and hold off rationalizing everything or linking to things already being done. Now and then, ask whether anyone knows how to structure this or what actions could come from it. But refrain from taking the lead in structuring, even if you feel everything is all over the place.

PATTERN: You have experience with the topic and immediately see the solutions. You tend to think others are slower in seeing the bigger picture and understanding how to solve it. You impose your solutions too quickly on the group, crippling them to see the possibilities themselves. This behavior nurtures your self-image of being a smart problem-solver.
COUNTERACT: Take the lead in ensuring the group doesn't jump to solutions yet. You might even create a "parking lot" for any solution that comes out too soon. Add your own solutions to the parking lot, leading by example.

Countering your patterns is a great way to make space for the unknown. It can also feel very liberating to become more conscious of the typical ways you think or behave. This practice can lead to a lot of personal growth.

MINING THE MINDS
If you don't feel comfortable working with your own patterns, another great way to depattern is by observing and exploring others' patterns. If you know the other individuals well, you probably already know what kind of thinking and behavior you can expect from them. If you don't know them very well, it is a valuable practice to try and identify their individual patterns.

Depending on their responsibilities, background, and personality, individuals might exhibit tendencies to control the conversation, deviate from the topic, remain stuck on their assumptions, hesitate to voice their opinions, avoid rigid thinking and imagine broadly but not concretely, exaggerate reality to influence others, take the lead, or follow certain people while disregarding the opinions of others. By talking less and observing more, you make ample space to explore the unknowns that other people can contribute.

Mining these minds involves activating thinking and behavior based on the patterns you observe – essentially calling upon someone's patterns. If someone tends to express themselves strongly to make their point, you can inquire about what makes them feel so passionately and ask about their past experiences related to the topic. When an expert shows a pattern of hesitation in sharing opinions, you can call upon their expertise whenever a factual or expert perspective is relevant to the conversation. If someone has authority and others tend to follow them, you can ask where they get their ideas from, who inspires them, or who they consider a credible source for better understanding a particular subject.

Playing on the patterns of others in a shared moment takes you out of your own patterns and makes ample space to observe new insights on a topic.

When your shared moment involves a good level of diversity, with participants from different teams, departments, or organizations, the varied beliefs underlying their thinking and doing bring a wealth of perspectives to understand the topic at hand. However, this diversity can only be leveraged if you remain an objective observer, playing on patterns to mine the minds of those involved. If you haven't invited people from "outside" your usual circle, playing on the known patterns of your team and mining their minds may yield less surprising insights. Inviting diversity into a shared moment enhances the results of "mining the minds."

Playing on patterns is a great way to leverage diversity while making space for unknowns to come to your attention. It is an effective method for avoiding being blinded by your own patterns.

HOW TO DEPATTERN USING SILENCE

Silence is the sound of creation, possessing the power to wipe everything clean. It can profoundly affect our minds and emotions, clearing mental clutter and facilitating an emotional reset. Silence is always the beginning and the end of something, existing before the storm and after. It de-identifies, unites, and embodies presence. Silence brings all our attention and energy to the moment – the birthplace of anything new.

THE CHANNEL

The channel draws inspiration from the concept of receiving your best ideas out of the blue. Insights dawn upon you, channeled from a creative field. The most brilliant ideas arise when you stop actively thinking about them – when you let go.

Whenever thought leaders participate in Q&A sessions, you'll notice they never rush into answers. There's a deliberate pause between the question and answer, as if they're allowing the question to sink in, creating space for the answer to arise. Often, people fear drawing a blank when put on the spot, so they prepare for anticipated questions and script their key messages. Ironically, the stress of adhering to a script can lead to coming up empty, and it rarely results in the most relevant answers for the moment. The most pertinent responses come from being fully present in the shared moment, as if the most relevant thoughts emerge out of the blue. Introducing brief pauses of silence allows for that kind of "inspirational presence," as if you're opening a channel to receive inspiration.

The key to practicing "the channel" is taking your time and pacing yourself:

WHENEVER YOU ARE CONFRONTED WITH A QUESTION, pause for a short moment of silence before answering it. Let the answer come to you instead of rushing into the first thing that comes to mind. Thank the person for the question. Let them know you are thinking about it, and take your time to answer.

WHENEVER A GROUP IS ADDRESSING A CHALLENGE OR QUESTION, avoid being the first to jump in and provide answers. Hold the space for others. Listen in and allow for all the information to sink in while making space for new thoughts to emerge.

WHENEVER YOU HAVE AN IDEA, only share it when the timing feels right in the conversation. Otherwise, don't share it and let it go to make space for other thoughts or listen to other people's thoughts.

WHENEVER A MEETING STARTS AND YOU ARE LEADING IT, make sure you don't take up all the space with introductions, agendas, and your thoughts about what should be achieved. Instead, keep the start short and get the others to start sharing their thoughts while you silently hold space for them.

WHENEVER A MEETING IS KICKED OFF BY SOMEONE ELSE, and the group starts discussing the first topic, avoid being the first one to talk. Instead, throw in some key questions and hold the space for others to answer.

WHENEVER YOU START SHARING YOUR THOUGHTS, create small pauses of silence before, during, and after you speak. This will allow you to be more present as you share your messages, feel more connected to everyone while interacting, and receive inspiration while you share.

By using silence to be much more conscious of what you are saying and when you speak, you reduce the chance of being blinded by unconscious patterns. Patterns manifest when you act on impulse.

THE SHIFT

Even when you share your thoughts, pacing yourself and utilizing small, silent pauses, you'll likely still identify with what you're expressing to some extent. Your opinion, always rooted in your beliefs, is an integral part of your perspective, even if it's your interpretation of someone else's viewpoint. It's still materialized by your mind and, therefore, a part of your identity.

To ensure you remain the observer, keeping the genius out of the bottle, it helps to return to silence as soon as you finish sharing or responding. If you participate in the discussion for too long, filling the space with your thoughts and making arguments to convince others of your points without reverting to being a silent observer, you risk identifying with your messages. Consequently, your unconscious patterns will likely start playing out.

Alternate, in a balanced way, between talking and observing silently in order to shift back from subject to object. Whenever you get too stuck on your beliefs while sharing them, you are squeezing yourself deeper and deeper into the bottle, unable to see the label. Silence will keep you out of the bottle, depatterning you, making space for the unknowns.

THE CLEANSE

The cleanse might be more of a group experiment. But it is initiated by a single person. It doesn't have to be the facilitator; it can be you.
The cleanse is using silence to close a topic or a trail of thoughts about a topic and make space for the next chapter, a different angle, or a new topic.

It is similar to the shift but on a group level. As a group, you take a moment of silence to allow the conversation to settle down and reflect on everything that has been said. It is a collective shift from subjectively engaging in conversation toward objectively reflecting on the outcome. Collectively letting go of the conversation and letting everything sink in as it stimulates collective depatterning.

The cleanse is particularly important when conversations become heated. It can be an invitation for everyone to take a minute of silence to let the conversation sink in. It could also take the shape of suggesting a couple of minutes of break before the conversation is continued. In a workshop, it can become an actual activity of reflection in silence. In a meeting, this would be overly structured and awkward. In this case, it can be a small break or a suggestion to take a minute to write some things down.

The key takeaway is that silence is a powerful way to let go. It allows you to remain the observer and make space instead of getting blinded by your patterns.

HOW TO DEPATTERN USING BLIND SPOTS

Blind spots are often generated by ego-driven behavioral patterns, as your mind can play tricks on you. It can create various stories justifying what is essentially an ego-driven need. Our evolutionary mechanisms for self-preservation, both physical and mental (identity), are sophisticated. We are not always aware of how our thinking and behavior can be traced back to our ego.

Depatterning using blind spots is essentially about creating more awareness of ego-driven patterns.

This type of depatterning is highly dependent on your state, more so than all the other depatterning practices. When you find yourself on the tension spectrum, your perspective becomes ego-driven. It's challenging to recognize ego if you're seeing the world through a filter of self-preservation. The triggers for a parasympathetic response are important enablers in recognizing these blind spots.

The practice is simple yet powerful.

Whenever you feel strongly about defending a certain point you're making, it means you're about to identify more with that point. It seems important to get everyone to agree with you. You're not making as much space for different perspectives; instead, you've decided to add more force to your own, convincing others to share your beliefs. In that case, when you feel that urge, you need to ask yourself three questions before proceeding:

1. Am I trying to gain personally from this, such as a reward, recognition, or validation? If I am, am I attempting to obtain it at the expense of others or the collective I am part of?
2. Is my pride or sense of self-worth shaken in any way that could make me defensive? Am I protecting an image I have of myself by avoiding or countering criticism or feedback?
3. Am I resisting the uncertainty of change, even though it could potentially provide new possibilities? Do I fear that change may put me in a vulnerable position?

There is nothing wrong with having to answer yes to any of these. As explained before, our ego is a magnificent mechanism for survival that we should cherish. On the other hand, it shouldn't take the upper hand and blind us. We should transcend it to achieve better connection and co-creation with others.

Whenever the answer is possibly yes to any of those questions, you can consciously decide to still continue making your point. Try to remain an observer, ready to make space for all kinds of responses from others. Or you can choose to not continue and let it go for now, feeling satisfied with being more aware of your blind spot.

If you are exceptionally brave and completely in tune with being vulnerable, you can come clean and tell everyone about your uncertainty around change, your concern about losing an opportunity for validation, or how something conflicts with your pride as context for a point you want to make. Depending on the group you are working with, this could either backfire or create a great deal of trust from others. Showing that level of vulnerability lets people know you are completely aware of your blind spots and are willing to not identify with your ego. That makes you far less threatening and a great person to co-create with.

GROUP EXPERIMENTS

Let's start again with the requirement for depatterning: being in the right state. Managing one's state can be done collectively. If you're aiming for depatterning as a facilitator, it's key to ensure that no one is in a stressed state, especially if your meetings or workshops require a significant amount of imagination and synergy from the participants.

SYNCHRONIZE STATES

Icebreakers, energizers, and mindsetters are common practices among experienced facilitators to get a group of people in the right mood. You do these exercises together as a group at the start of a workshop or between workshop activities to prepare for the upcoming co-creative activities. It can generate some fun. It often involves physical activities, which always have great benefits for workshop participants. But the most important benefit is synchronizing the group. Synchronizing means we are helping them become a collective, tuning into the moment and connecting with each other, aligning their thinking, movement, and even state.

Synchronizers are a specific type of energizer or mindsetter that has a synchronizing effect on the group. They help us loosen up on our personal truths and consider other beliefs to jointly arrive at an evolved interpretation of things.

STATE SYNCHRONIZERS, which focus on collectively synchronizing body and mind, can be particularly effective in helping a group of co-creators trigger their parasympathetic nervous systems and manage an aligned state. Among the most powerful exercises for synchronizing a group of people are State Synchronizers that utilize breathwork.

If you want to practice a breathwork technique with a group to synchronize their states, ensure that you are very familiar with the technique and have a clear intention about the kind of state you would like to achieve. Participants who have never practiced breathwork may struggle with longer breath holds and overly slow breathing. A feeling of air hunger can trigger their sympathetic nervous system and cause stress. Some breathwork techniques can put people to sleep, while others can energize them.

When synchronizing participants' states in a workshop environment, your aim should be to balance their autonomic nervous system right in the middle between "sympathetic" and "parasympathetic" – what we have previously called the "Relaxed Focused State."

The best-known breathing technique for achieving a Relaxed Focused State is BOX BREATHING: *inhale* for four counts, *hold* for four counts, *exhale* for four counts, *hold* for four counts; repeat ten times. Align your counts with a second or even slightly less to avoid a shortage of breath among inexperienced participants.

Box Breathing is always a safe technique to apply when synchronizing state. Any other breathing technique that starts from a simple four-count slow breathing pattern is a perfect foundation to build upon. You can add instructions to make gestures while breathing in and out to intensify the exercise. Additionally, you can instruct participants to breathe into the heart area and evoke emotions of appreciation. When generated authentically on demand, such emotions can strongly affect people's states.

While breathing is a powerful synchronizer, everyone experiences it differently. Always ensure that you don't push people to or beyond their limits. It is better to err on the side of caution and apply breathing techniques that are easy and comfortable for everyone.

GROUP DEPATTERNING

A group has shared thinking and behavioral patterns, and individuals have their own patterns. Becoming aware of your personal patterns is more of a personal experiment. As a group, you can experiment with some techniques that can disrupt patterns of engaging with each other without being aware of the type of patterns. These techniques prompt the participants to think differently, lifting them out of their typical way of collaborating.

GROUP DEPATTERNING TACTICS

1. Take a stand

Divide the group into two or more "parties," each with opposing viewpoints on a topic. Each party prepares its extreme perspective for a debate, gathering its strongest arguments. Facilitate the confrontation. Each party presents and defends its viewpoints, challenged by the other parties. Following the debate, each party has to indicate common ground, aiming to reach a consensus where possible. This process stimulates critical thinking, encourages dialogue, and ultimately leads to deeper insights for informed decision-making.

2. Devil's advocate

When a group has worked together for many years, they may become too comfortable with each other to effectively challenge ideas. Assigning the role of a "Devil's Advocate" can change this dynamic by mandating that person to challenge group thinking and ensure critical analysis. To keep the process productive and maintain a positive energy in the room, it's important to establish clear rules and assign the right people as "challengers." The Devil's Advocate's job is to highlight blind spots and risks during conversation, fostering a more comprehensive understanding of the topic at hand. This tactic is most effective when used in smaller breakout discussions.

3. Outside-in

By infusing a co-creative session with personal stories gathered from credible key stakeholders at the right time, preferably after the group has formed their initial conclusion, the preconceived interpretations and habitual thinking can be disrupted. Surprising the participants with unexpected testimonials on a topic from credible sources will make them more aware of their own biases. The raw, unfiltered stories should evoke emotional responses, making them more impactful than polished reports. Bringing in outside-in information in a disruptive way can foster richer, more nuanced conversations and insights.

4. Use past mistakes

To ensure past errors are not overlooked during creative brainstorming sessions, the co-creators can be prompted to reflect on significant past mistakes and imagine their potential impact when applied to current challenges. Participants are reminded of the importance of integrating these lessons into their new approach by vividly exploring the consequences of applying past mistakes again to current challenges and their lingering effects. This process keeps past mistakes at the forefront of their minds, fostering awareness of their potential impact on new solutions and guiding the evolution away from past mistakes.

5. Share with care

This tactic is about shaping the sharing by suggesting a particular type of audience or situation to keep in mind. "Share with care" encourages participants to share their thoughts in a way that provokes responses from the other participants. For example, by sharing it as if they are explaining it to their grandparents, keeping it low on technological features and fancy gimmicks. Or explain it as if you are explaining it to your kids, investors, or victims. It can also go beyond addressing an audience by taking on a role or imagining a certain situation. For example, explain it as a dictator, as an activist, as an optimist vs. a pessimist, as if we live in 2050, after a worldwide ecological disaster, as if the internet doesn't exist, or as if AI has taken over.

6. *Make the sell*

Another way to shape interpretations and encourage sharing is by asking a group of participants to make a sales pitch. They should prepare the most concise description of the "what" and the reason(s) why other participants might not buy into it. Additionally, they should identify the three top "why" items that counter those potential doubts and hesitations.

Here's the twist: when asking the participants to share, instruct them to only present the "what" and the top-of-mind reasons why others might doubt or hesitate to accept it. Then, ask the audience to respond with various arguments that counter the presented potential doubts and hesitations. Finally, have the presenter(s) share their own top "why" items to address the imagined doubts and hesitations and compare them with the ones presented by the audience.

7. *Rise and fall*

This tactic challenges conventional thinking by emphasizing the importance of considering both the peak and decline phases when envisioning new possibilities. It prompts discussions about sustainability, triggers controversy, and fosters deeper understanding of the durability of the value delivered by an organization. By exploring the lifecycle of ideas, products, or relationships, participants gain insights into resilience, innovation, and the expiration date of relevancy. This approach encourages flexibility and humility, recognizing that everything has a lifecycle, including the best ideas.

8. *Opposites attract*

This tactic works best when you have two clearly different and relevant perspectives in the room. For example, customers and employees, CEO/C-suite and people on the "work floor," men and women, Boomer and Gen Z, etc. Set the scene for a controversial situation related to the topic of the workshop or meeting. For example:

Perspectives: Customers vs. employees
Imaginary situation: More gets charged at the end of service delivery compared to the initial proposal without any budget updates or alerts during delivery.

Perspectives: CEO/C-suite vs. "work floor"
Imaginary situation: People aren't proactively informed and/or are not consulted before a radical new change is implemented, which results in restrictions on how holidays can be taken due to changes in legislation.

Perspectives: Men vs. women
Imaginary situation: When it comes time for the yearly performance review, the performance of women who took maternity leave is compared to those who didn't.

Perspectives: Babyboomer vs. Gen Z
Imaginary situation: Long-tenured or senior employees in the company always get the last say when things are decided due to their experience.

When the situation is interpreted by both parties, fully understood and alive in their imaginations, they transform themselves into becoming the other party. Both parties step into the other party's shoes and formulate what they would think, do, and feel in that situation.

When the other party expresses where they got it right and wrong, it usually becomes a very vivid and enlightening conversation for both parties, resulting in a deeper understanding of each other.

The tactics mentioned above are just a few examples of how to depattern group collaboration. These tactics make space for looking at things through different perspectives and drawing conclusions in unconventional ways. As a facilitator, you can design your own depatterning tactics by inventing different setups, assigning roles or mandates, and changing the rules of engagement. For example, you can alter the language used to achieve better and more unconventional outcomes.

To enhance the impact of these tactics in meetings or workshops, ensure that you invite a diverse group of participants from different teams, departments, or even organizations. Additionally, use silence as a tool to allow for deep reflection and to pause and reboot discussions when needed.

Dear Diary,

I've been doing better since the last time I wrote. I got to a point where I was done feeling restless. I caught myself thinking unnecessary anxious thoughts as if it had become a habit. I couldn't make sense of why I was having these thoughts about things going wrong, people not taking up their responsibilities, management not being supportive, my kids not caring about household chores, etc. Reflecting upon these thoughts, I realized there was absolutely no reason for me to be more concerned or critical than before. I realized it wasn't the outer world that became more challenging. I got stuck in a state conducive to such obsessive thinking. Being on the edge most of the time. With this realization, I decided to observe my thoughts much more, not getting carried away by them. I stopped believing all of them. I stopped identifying with them. I got to know myself in a way I never did before. It was so insightful, to notice thoughts and feelings bubbling up without being overtaken by them. I even started seeing patterns in other people's talking and behavior. Things I had never realized because I was too stuck in my own thinking before. It feels like I am developing a sixth sense for patterns. The beauty is if you see the patterns, you can consciously start playing with them. Yesterday, I was having lunch with a colleague who loves to gossip about other colleagues, and I always used to go along with it, being triggered by her juicy stories and opinions. This time, I decided to play with it and respond differently. When she brought up her first gossip about Marie, I responded with a story about how Marie was such an amazing source of support during my latest project. I kept repeating the same thing, bringing up something really nice about a person she started gossiping about. Her attempts to have a juicy, gossipy conversation with me slowed down. Eventually, they transformed into an open, very vulnerable sharing of the complicated relationship with her mom. Something that had never come up before, but now there seemed to be space for her to talk about it. I also noticed how powerful it is to not speak my thoughts on impulse but just observe what is being said and finding my moment to share something. Even when the urge to respond was so strong, especially when the urge was strong, I replaced the talking with silent observing, letting go of the things I wanted to share. Playing around with my habits has lifted my spirits. It is a new me. A very conscious me. A very, very curious me, relieved of the burden of a running mind. It gives me energy, although some fatigue lately has made it hard to sustain my attention in the endless series of meetings throughout each day.

Your Vaganaut

CHAPTER 6. ANCHORING

IT'S TWO O'CLOCK in the afternoon. We're in a small meeting room, set up classroom style. I am delivering my "Prepare for Successful Co-Creation" course to six diverse people. A young new hire (I'm not sure she is enjoying the course), a few co-creation enthusiasts (eating up everything I'm saying), a critical thinker in the front row (convinced she already knows this stuff), and the person promoting this course, my contact in the organization (who currently has a thousand-yard stare). Let's call him Bart.

I have been delivering this training as part of a facilitation training program for a while in this large organization. This course in the program is focused on teaching people how to strategically prepare a workshop they will facilitate. In the morning, we deep dive into framing a workshop, investigating hooks, goals, and the diversity of the workshop team. In the afternoon, we explore how to build a good program of activities and prepare for pitfalls.

At this moment, I am explaining the concept of opening and closing activities in a workshop, as well as instructions and conclusions. Amid my explanations, I get distracted by the stare in Bart's eyes. His eyes are half open, and he is wearing an unnatural grin. No movement. Like a statue, leaning a bit to the right. Maybe even a bit too far to the right, as if he might tip over any moment. At first, it doesn't seem abnormal, and I continue explaining. I glance at him a few more times. There is no movement, just the same stare. Is he falling asleep? Thoughts rush through my mind as I realize he's actually entering the land of nod. Am I dragging this out too long? Am I losing everyone's attention, repeating myself too much, or explaining the content too theoretically? Everyone else seems to be listening closely.

I decide to call on him, "Hey Bart, are you still with us?" He doesn't respond and still has a grin, his eyes half closed.

I ask again, "Bart, are you still here?"

He suddenly opens his eyes widely and looks surprised, trying to figure out what just happened. As he realizes he'd been falling asleep, he quickly responds, "No, no, yes, yes, I was reflecting upon what you were saying and got lost in my thoughts. Carry on, interesting stuff."

I give him a warm smile to make sure he doesn't feel bad about it and announce a short break for everyone.

Bart had been distracted by his watch and smartphone notifications throughout the morning. As he is promoting this course and providing the budget to deliver the program across departments, I need to ensure he is still convinced of the program's value. A bit concerned, I ask him during the break if everything is okay and whether the course content is engaging enough. He apologizes for nodding off and explains he has an intense week with a lot going on. I ask him whether he is still okay to stay to the end. Luckily, he confirms, but he just might need to step out now and then to call some people. That is fine with me.

I am not yet completely at ease with Bart's response. The previous sessions went great, but maybe there is a blind spot I missed. And so, I ask Bart what he liked most about the morning's learnings. His answer is vague and hesitant, and he misses the essential messages I'd weaved into the course. I decide to let it go and continue with delivering the course, planning to ask for feedback from a couple of participants afterward.

The feedback was positive. Some were even very excited as they had learned things they specifically needed to best facilitate an upcoming workshop. I felt relief.

It also got me thinking about how people manage their attention and make space. Bart's attention was divided across multiple things in his life at the moment. Trying to tackle them reactively wore him out. It's impossible to handle different things at the same time. We might feel we're efficiently multi-tasking, but we are actually rapidly switching our focus between various topics and tasks, not allowing for one thing to get sufficient attention. Bart was exhausted after a day, probably a week, of reactive multi-tasking. His memory didn't work that well during the course. Hence, he couldn't reproduce any learnings, his creativity was lost, and he probably suffered from lingering stress.

The other participants stuck with the program. Despite the after-lunch dip in energy, they were engaged and focused until the end. They didn't get distracted by notifications on their devices, nor did they allow their minds to jump onto different topics unrelated to the course. They anchored their attention to the course again and again.

ARE WE FACING A FOCUS PROBLEM?

Equipped with smartwatches and smartphones, we check our devices continuously during the day, from morning to evening. Twitter (or X) gained popularity with its brevity, with messages initially of 140 characters and now 280 characters. TikTok gained popularity by providing video content that is created and consumed quickly. A TikTok video is 15–60 seconds in length. Snapchat provides ephemeral content, the ability to send "snaps" – photos or videos – that disappear after they've been viewed by the recipient. Facebook, LinkedIn, and other social media channels get people hooked thanks to the mechanics of instant gratification. Content is available everywhere and in small bite sizes. With Spotify and Apple Music, you have any song you want, while in the past, you had to buy an artist's album and play it from the beginning to the end. Most people are engaged with socials all the time, quickly switching between messages and between channels, being stingy with their attention, and seeking instant gratification. There are even books written about how to "speak emoji," helping you replace your boringly long sentences with snappy symbols. 📚✍️🔄💬😄, 🆘🔄\🔤🚫🤭…💊🔖🤩.

We train our brains for short-term satisfaction, distractibility, chunk-sized pieces of information, reduced information retention, and constant connectivity. The more we expose ourselves to this way of information processing and interaction, the harder it gets to focus consistently on one thing for long.

Anchoring is a way to keep your attention on a moment of co-creation. It is the fourth tenet of making space, and it can help us train our focus and lengthen our attention span.

This chapter explains four ways to anchor your attention to make space for a moment of co-creation for as long as necessary. They are inspired by Nir Eyal's book, *Hooked: How to Build Habit-Forming Products*, and his framework for creating products and services designed to form habits in users. In his book, Nir Eyal explains four core principles to get people to invest and keep investing their attention in a product or service:

1. TRIGGER: Initiate user action through cues that can be external (like notifications) or evolve into internal (like emotions).
2. ACTION: Make the behavior easy to perform following the trigger, aiming for simplicity and convenience.
3. VARIABLE REWARD: Provide unpredictable rewards that satisfy different user needs, keeping engagement high.
4. INVESTMENT: Encourage users to invest time, data, or effort, enhancing their future interactions with the product and fostering repeated use.

This framework has inspired a lot of app builders to develop apps that hijack your attention. Ironically, you can use the same principles to make space. The perfect counter-attack. Fighting fire with fire.

As your trigger to keep your attention in check, you can use your hook (Chapter 4). The second principle, ease of use, comes from acknowledging the beauty of the situation. Reward is borne of appreciating the synergy. And finally, investment is covered by recognizing the progress being made. To sum it up in a new framework:

1. Anchor to your hook
2. Anchor to the moment
3. Anchor to synergy
4. Anchor to your progress

Let's explore these four ways of anchoring more in depth before turning them into practices.

ANCHOR TO YOUR HOOK

Human attention is limited. Each person's capacity to maintain focus is different. It takes mental energy to remain focused, using your working memory. Depleted mental resources can lead to a decrease in attentional capacity. Lack of sleep, too much multi-tasking, and stress are some factors that impact our capacity to remain focused.

Remaining focused on one task or topic isn't about stretching your focus. Your focus will naturally decrease after a while. It is a matter of refocusing again and again as long as it is necessary. This part might be hard if you've trained your brain for short content processing and instant gratification.

It is a matter of refocusing again and again.

Research has explored the differences in attention span, measured in seconds, between Generation Z and Millennials. However, the precise results of this research on the length of sustained focus before needing to refocus are irrelevant. What matters more is the capability and willingness to refocus attention. Just like training for strength or endurance, refocusing attention requires effort. As your brain adapts to the new demands, it will become more efficient in using energy to focus and refocus. Attention span is not a generational issue, just as fitness or capability levels are not inherently determined by one's generation. It is a personal capability that can be trained and developed, like any other skill.

People who haven't trained their brains for refocusing have brains that wander all the time. It's a multi-tasking brain that is all over the place; it craves continuous new stimuli. These people can be from any generation or background. They will have a hard time making space for anything.

Whatever kind of brain you have trained, it will always selectively filter and prioritize incoming sensory information based on relevance and importance. This selective process helps us focus on what's most important while ignoring irrelevant or distracting stimuli. We can only attend to a limited amount of information at once.

Refocusing comes down to amplifying the importance of your task to help your brain select this task alone to focus on. It is as easy as that. It is also as hard as that. If you haven't found your groove with a hook for doing the task and the task or topic still seems boring or irrelevant, you will have difficulty refocusing. You will struggle with anchoring your attention to keep the space open for the task.

Some kids can play Fortnite for 12 hours straight, but they can't focus 2 minutes on their math exercises. I can spend hours reading about human psychology but have a harder time staying focused when reading investment strategies. When I found my hook related to investing in a holiday home in a sunny place, I could easily refocus to learn about investment strategies in real estate.

Your hook will allow you to open space for something. It will also help you keep the space open whenever you need to refocus. "Anchoring to your hook" means keeping your hook in mind. You keep it on the horizon to easily remind yourself why you want to stay focused in the moment. The power of your hook is the emotional connection you have to it. That's why we investigated how you can resonate strongly with your hook in Chapter 4.

Finding your trigger in your thinking, feeling, and/or doing, understanding how it matches with who you want to be and how it supports how you want to be perceived, creates a strong emotional hook. That kind of hook will anchor your attention for as long as it takes. It will help your brain select the shared moment as the most relevant source of information. It will help you refocus, whether you have a brain that can easily refocus or not.

Anchoring your attention with a strong hook allows for deep creative space. The one that elevates collaboration to co-creation.

ANCHOR TO THE MOMENT
Even though your hook might be strong, reminding yourself of it again and again to anchor your attention can become tedious. You don't want to keep playing your favorite song until it becomes elevator music. Milking the cow dry. Eating your favorite dessert until you never want to see it again. Your brain will tend to look at other things and consider them more important and relevant.

For example, you receive an unexpected and urgent message from your manager, during your moment of co-creation. Your manager is the person who also approves your current holiday request and is the same person who will evaluate your performance next month. Based on your emotions drawn from your previous experiences and learnings related to working with your manager, your brain might decide now to first respond to the message rather than stick with the moment of co-creation. Even despite your strong hook. This happens *especially* when the cow is dry.

Some variety in the way you anchor will help you keep your attention in the moment despite other seemingly relevant information popping up out of nowhere. It doesn't have to be a notification; it might also be a distracting thought associated with something somebody just said. For example, "I did my taxes yesterday; they were long overdue." You might start wandering off, thinking about whether you have done them, whether it is too late, what the consequences are, etc.

There are many ways to lose focus. A good anchoring strategy is necessary to sustain it, and variety is key. One way to add variety is to anchor to "the moment." That means you use your appreciation of the moment to keep your attention on it. Your switch will already have helped you to "want" the moment to happen. The feeling of appreciation combined with your intention (coming from your switch) is solid ground to anchor into.

Your appreciation of the moment can come from all kinds of perspectives on the moment:

- You appreciate the time and effort that the other(s) is (are) investing in this moment.
- You appreciate the feeling of connecting in person and the opportunity to really dig in.
- You appreciate the setting of the moment, nice coffee, calming situation, exciting view, etc.
- You appreciate who you can be for these people, your added value, your support, etc.
- You appreciate the attention you are receiving, the acknowledgment, the appreciation.

Appreciating the moment is a great way to anchor your attention and keep making space for it to happen, shunning other attention grabbers.

You are even getting a double scoop! Extra cheese on your pizza! By anchoring to and appreciating the moment, you set the stage for great depatterning. Doing so will relax you into the moment, fuel your connection to the moment and the other people, and allow for vulnerability. You can more easily let go of fixed mindsets and become more curious about what this moment can offer. This depatterning bonus leads us to another way of anchoring your attention: anchoring to synergy.

ANCHOR TO SYNERGY

Switching and your hook will lay a perfect foundation to build on for anchoring. Anchoring into both the moment and your hook can happen like the tides. Emotions related to the shared moment during your switch and finding your hook can be brought up again regularly to keep your attention at bay and the space open. They work in unison to allow for great co-creation.

> *By anchoring to and appreciating the moment, you set the stage for great depatterning.*

Co-creation in itself can then also become solid ground to anchor into. You can anchor your attention with your curiosity for novelty, different perspectives, and deeper understanding – if you can rule out the fear and discomfort of not having all the answers. You can keep your attention anchored to the perspectives others are sharing. You can make space by wanting to explore the secrets other people might reveal, shedding a different light on a topic that deepens your understanding.

You can also anchor your attention to the shared responsibility that comes from co-creation. The co-ownership of moving it forward. The ideas others bring to the table to jointly create a new reality. If you can rule out the resistance to taking on more work and the resistance to change, you can allow for a feeling of companionship and community. You can keep your attention anchored in the solutions and approaches others share. You can make space by wanting to explore the actions this moment results in.

Anchoring your attention to the emerging opinions and ideas out of curiosity is anchoring into synergy. While anchoring to your hook and the moment can easily become second nature, anchoring into synergy is more deliberate. You have to deliberately explore other minds and nurture your curiosity without letting any concerns or discomfort take the upper hand.

Whenever people feel they aren't listened to and conversations grow irrelevant to them, they become more easily distracted. They might even look for distractions to disconnect from the moment. The idea of anchoring into synergy is that you deliberately never stop exploring the synergy to find growth and belonging during the shared moment. This keeps your attention in the moment, and it leads to a sense of progress. Sometimes it takes persistence to finally see the beauty of the synergy happening. It is rarely delivered to you on a silver platter. Whether you can see it or not depends on your willingness and your curiosity. When you see it, it is a perfect anchor to sustain your attention to find more of it.

> *Never stop exploring the synergy to find growth and belonging.*

ANCHOR TO YOUR PROGRESS

In the end, there is only one thing everyone wants from co-creation. It doesn't matter if it is a small co-creative moment in the form of a meeting or an extensive co-creative workshop. We all want the same thing. Progress. Arriving at a better place than when we arrived.

People generally dislike meetings because of the lack of progress. Meetings that don't amount to anything. That don't lead to a better starting point. They feel like a waste of time. Meetings are often not thought through or adequately prepared, or they don't take into account all the necessary perspectives, etc. A lack of progress, despite having to invest your time, leads to meeting cultures where no space is really created. It is collaboration but not co-creation. In such meeting cultures, people have a hard time keeping their full focus in the meeting. They have a predisposition to not wasting their time and energy too much. You will immediately recognize these cultures – with all the laptops open and participants answering emails while being in a conversation. That kind of meeting culture has little co-creative potential.

Assuming by now you are into **switching**, creating a **hook** for yourself, and becoming **conscious of your thinking** and behavioral patterns, you are on your way to making space each time you have a shared moment.

You might already notice that even if a meeting is not properly prepared and/or randomly set up, making space for it already allows for more value to come from it. It is turning what was a moment of collaboration into co-creation. There is progress to anchor to if you are willing to see and capture it.

Anchoring to progress, just like anchoring to synergy, is a deliberate act. You have to look for it. To anchor to synergy, you have to be *curious*. To anchor to progress, you have to have *zeal*. Whenever you feel something important has been achieved with those involved, you can anchor your attention and even the attention of others by ensuring that achievement is properly captured for everyone to understand. This is literally a moment of anchoring the co-creation for progress. Navigating the co-creation maze, leaving breadcrumbs of brilliance in your wake.

> *To anchor to progress, you have to have zeal.*

You can anchor to progress by yourself or as a group. If you anchor by yourself, it often needs a short moment of silence. A pause, as explained in the previous chapter. It is a moment where you let things sink in and capture the essential elements, the golden nuggets, coming from the co-creation. Because the resulting value of the co-creation is now clear, it is easy to keep your attention in the moment. Usually, it doesn't remain a quick, personal, silent reflection because there is a lot of merit in repeating the essential conclusions with everyone involved to keep everyone's attention in the moment. Then, the co-creation will feel valuable to everyone and worth the time and effort. This group anchoring into progress will help everyone make space for the moment to continue.

After a couple of progress anchors, a similar effect to the "investment" component in Nir Eyal's framework will occur. All participants will feel they have invested significant effort and accomplished substantial progress, becoming advocates for the desired outcome. This sense of investment will motivate them to remain focused until the goal is achieved.

Anchoring to your hook, the moment, and synergy are individual reflections that take place during the shared moment. Anchoring to your progress can happen individually, but it has many benefits when also practiced in a group.

Let's make this practical so you can start experimenting with it personally and in groups.

ANCHORING
Experiments

PERSONAL EXPERIMENTS

This practice aims to refocus whenever your attention is drifting off to other things and to train yourself to refocus, which will grow easier over time. Anchoring will help your brain prioritize the shared moment over other incoming information.

MY PERSONAL PRACTICE
Before a shared moment, I try to make sure there is no resistance and that my intention of who I want to be is clear in my mind. I also reflect upon why this moment matters to me. I go with the hook that has the strongest "pull." It takes just a couple of minutes to get my head straight before I go in.

Then, anchoring during a meeting flows naturally. Whenever I notice my mind wandering, I take a moment to recap or connect the dots to organize the content of the conversation for myself. But also to ensure I am still on the same page as the others (s). It pulls my attention back to continue the moment. It might even help the others as well. Whenever I notice someone else's attention decreasing, I often decide to do a quick rephrasing to check whether I understood everything correctly. I also ask that person whether they have a similar take, to pull their attention back. Depending on my hook, I might also add how it matters to me when I am rephrasing, doing a recap, or connecting the dots to show by example that the conversation has my full attention as it is important to me. If I do this a couple of times, the others start feeling that it also matters to them. At least, it matters to them that this matters to me, which also keeps their attention in the moment.

Depatterning is always on my mind when I have a shared moment. I value curiosity about other perspectives a lot. That mindset leads me to use a lot of silences and active listening. Exploring the depths of other people's ideas and opinions keeps my attention anchored. Because I tend to depattern my thoughts and learn new insights at every shared moment, I don't have to deliberately "explore" to sustain my attention. If you are not that much into depatterning, it would be a good idea to install an intention during your switch to at least explore as much as you speak during conversations. Deliberately asking more questions out of curiosity will help to keep the space open.

Anchoring happens naturally when I am energized and attentive. There are moments when I haven't had a good night's sleep or it's been a long day. Being tired makes it very hard not to get distracted. When I notice my mind wandering more than usual, I remind myself of "more" (see below) to make sure I deliberately organize and explore. I might even write down my hook with some keywords somewhere visible on top of the page or in my notebook. That helps me relate the organizing and exploring to my hook whenever it feels relevant. This approach always keeps my attention on the moment despite fatigue. It nurtures my ability to refocus and trains my brain to easily refocus going forward.

Doing one thing at a time makes you more effective and allows you to use your full capacity in the moment. Anchoring practices can make you happier at work, more connected, creative, and relaxed.

For anchoring to become second nature, starting with a spontaneous, easy approach is important. As you consciously anchor more and more and experience its effect, you will begin to anchor automatically. I think most people naturally do some kind of anchoring when they need to sustain their focus for more extended periods of time.

When I realized I was anchoring during meetings, I decided to do it more consciously in order to turn it into a personal practice. To make sure I didn't jinx something that worked well by trying to do it more consciously, I looked for an easy-to-use guide to help myself anchor consciously. What works better than a good acronym? Using some acro-brilliance to turn a mouthful into a strong word, I came up with "MORE." That stuck with me and was easy to remember because the idea behind anchoring is to get more of the shared moment and more co-creation.

M – Moment (anchor to the moment)
O – Organize (anchor to progress)
R – Reason (anchor to the hook)
E – Explore (anchor to synergy)

To have more of the shared moment, bringing your attention back to it again and again, you have to appreciate the moment, organize the outcomes for progress, keep your reason for taking part top of mind, and explore the others' perspectives.

MOMENT

By appreciating the moment in your switch and setting your intention, you have already created an appreciative association with that moment. Anchoring to the moment is trying to keep that appreciative feeling alive. We've already discussed different perspectives on the moment to feel appreciation. If you keep "MORE" in mind with the "M" for "Moment," it helps you to keep looking for the beauty of the moment. Or the silver lining if conversations are difficult.

Remaining appreciative of the moment fuels your motivation to deliberately anchor your attention to synergy and progress. In other words, it keeps you motivated to organize and explore even if the moment is challenging.

ORGANIZE

A conversation happens as a series of bell curves, like flares or waves of conversation bubbling up and tapering off again. Each flare is an angle on the topic being discussed. The flares overlap and have different curve shapes. Some are higher, some are wider, meaning some conversations trigger more voices, and some are dragged out longer. It takes quite a bit of mental energy to ride these waves of conversation. You might fall off the surfboard now and then, getting distracted by things outside the conversation. You can also tumble and get lost in the waves, not knowing what direction they're rolling in.

Conversational waves

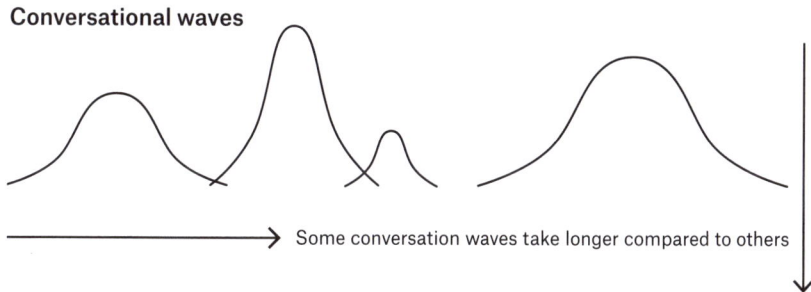

Some conversation waves take longer compared to others

Some conversation waves have more energy, participation, and emotions

To anchor yourself in an organized way to progress, you can take a moment to:
- Recap what has been said.
- Connect what has been said to a previous conclusion in an earlier conversation.
- Rephrase statements in a different way for better understanding.

Pausing at the end of a curve to organize conversational content in one of the above ways provides a feeling of progress. Doing this often will help conversational waves head in a given direction and not toss about in all kinds of divergent directions. Participants will easily lose focus if a conversation is all over the place. Conversely, when a conversation seems to go somewhere interesting, it is easier for everyone to stay focused. When participants often take a moment to organize and anchor their attention to the conversation's progress, the curves become higher. There is more resonance.

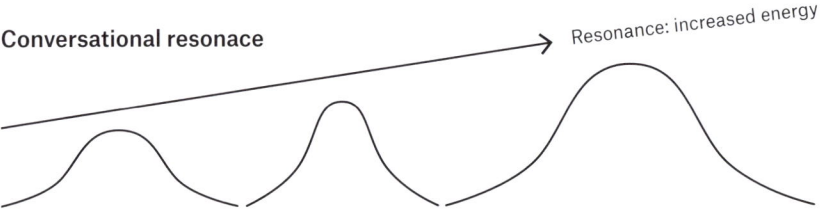

Conversational resonace

Resonance: increased energy

REASON

The "R" in "MORE" is your reason for taking part in the moment. Your hook. Finding a compelling hook before the moment starts helps you keep your attention in the moment. Anchoring into the hook is trying to keep that "pull" of the hook alive. The stronger your initial emotion related to your hook, the easier it gets to call upon that emotion.

It helps to try and relate the progress-anchoring, "Organize," to your hook to keep the pull alive. This means that whenever you recap or connect the dots, you can try to do this within the context of your hook.

Imagine that your hook for the moment is getting buy-in from different stakeholders. When you take a moment to recap what has been said, anchoring in progress, you can weave in the needs of these stakeholders and assess how much these needs are being met. Anchoring to progress within the context of your hook fuels your emotional connection to the moment.

In the same way, it also helps to try and relate the synergy-anchoring to your hook. This means that when asking questions to explore someone's perspective, you can search for questions also relevant to your hook.

Imagine your hook is getting everyone up to speed, aligned, and excited about a project to start a partnership. When you listen actively to someone's perspective on the partnership, you can ask specific questions about their part in the future collaboration. This feeds into your hook of creating alignment and excitement and is fueled by your curiosity to get more perspective.

A strong hook from the start will easily stay top of mind and keep you motivated to organize and explore. But not every hook will be as compelling. You might have a lighter, less emotional hook for different meetings throughout the day. Then your appreciation for the moment, after switching, needs to keep you motivated to organize and explore.

EXPLORE

As we've seen, a conversation's waves, or bell curves, can move in different directions. The waves can also be short, overlapping, and numerous. A conversation that happens erratically – we've all had them. In this case, people aren't actively listening to each other. They are randomly opening up new, different angles without finishing previous angles properly (overlap). This kind of conversation takes a lot of mental energy and can't be sustained for long.

To anchor yourself in an exploratory way into synergy, you deliberately look for interesting new interpretations from others to deep dive into. Instead of adding new angles on the topic, you ask questions to better understand what the others are saying.

The quality of your questions determines the quality of the conversation and the strength of your anchoring. Ask from curiosity, not from validation of your thoughts. Ask open instead of leading questions. The others will start sharing stories instead of short answers. The waves become wider.

Anchoring your attention by organizing and exploring will obviously increase the energy. The conversational waves become wider and higher. Resonance increases. Brains become more aligned or "coupled."

You are making space for a conversation to become more qualitative, keeping your attention in check.

Deliberate anchoring needs motivation. You increased your motivation already by switching and finding your hook before the moment started. It can be fueled by anchoring to the moment and the hook while you are in the moment, holding on to the feeling the switch and hook gave you.

GROUP EXPERIMENTS

As mentioned before, anchoring to progress is a valuable group exercise. Organizing conversational content often as a group keeps everyone on track. As a facilitator, you wouldn't summarize or connect the dots for the group yourself, but you can suggest a participant try and capture the conclusions for the group to consider. Otherwise, you might bias the outcome of the conversations. This is a great way to keep everyone's attention on the activity when people start disconnecting. It is absolutely crucial to install a group anchoring moment *at the end of an activity in your workshop* so they can find closure before moving on to the next thing.

At the end of each activity, taking a moment to summarize the outcome and ensuring everyone agrees will instill a sense of progress and belonging among the participants. With this shared understanding, they'll be more focused and receptive to instructions for the next step, knowing the journey is progressing toward the established goals.

End-of-activity closing moments can happen in different ways:

– Ask a participant to recap.
– Ask everyone to share their takeaways in a sharing round.
– Ask the participants to talk with their neighbor about the most important conclusions and have them share them, duo by duo.
– Ask the group where the most progress was made, in popcorn style.
– Ask everyone to write down what they will keep top of mind as they move into the next activity.

Participants almost always feel like taking a breather at the end of an activity. If fatigue sets in, this is the moment when they start getting distracted by other things. Especially when installing a break between the next activity, collectively anchoring to progress will be very effective in keeping them in the game.

If you have asked them to reflect on their hook at the start of your meeting or workshop, you can also ask them to anchor to progress, recapping the most important outcomes and relating them to their hooks. If the outcome matches what matters to them well, the anchoring will be even stronger during the closure. The feeling of progress will be stronger and will keep them hooked.

Dear Diary,

Someone said something a couple of days ago that made me stop and think. It was so simple yet profound. She said, "I see everyone around me trying to have some control over their careers, their relationships, their finances, and even their kids. Heck! I catch myself trying to control my life. But you know what is so funny? In the end, there is really only one thing we can control. And we leave it up for grabs! We can control what deserves our attention in life. But we waste it away by allowing a lot of useless crap to grab our attention. Things that even make us feel bad. Do you know what the most ironic thing about it is? It is not our achievements in our finances, relationships, careers, or the desired behavior of our kids that makes us happy; it is the way we perceive and pay attention to these aspects. The way we pay attention to things in our life makes up our life, and yet we let our erratic thinking minds or silly social channels hijack it." This message came at the right time for me. It resonates so, so much. The reason why I am enjoying my life again at the moment, even though it has never been so busy, is because I am directing my attention more deliberately to connect more deeply with myself and others, allowing for serendipity to present its gifts to me. It is such an epiphany to me. How crazy is it to give away the one thing I can control in life? The one thing that can bring immediate life quality every minute of every day. I own my attention. I decide which thoughts, which content, which moments deserve my attention, and why. Now that I am consciously directing and sustaining my attention, I have even stopped watching commercials and decided not to fill up my life with world news. I decided to spend more time with other people, listening to their ideas and getting a glimpse of everyone's emotional world. And I spend more time with me. It is my garden; I decide which flowers will grow in it.

Your Vaganaut

CHAPTER 7.
INCEPTION

THE DOORBELL RINGS, and I look toward the garden through our 12-meter square window. It is one of the key features of our house: a steel-framed 3-meter by 4-meter triple-glass window that was installed with an impressive, long-armed glazing crane, also called a glassworker, about seven years ago. I remember watching the installation and thinking it would be impossible to replace that window once our house was finished.

I see her running toward the window. She is still a puppy but already huge in size. The doorbell has always triggered her. I wasn't able to change its Pavlovian effect with treats and encouragement. Her steps look clunky. Her paws seem too big, even though her size is significant. She runs as if she doesn't yet know how to properly move this big dog body; her huge paws are swinging all over the place.

As I watch her running toward the window from the other side, my facial expression changes as if I am expecting a painful blow to the face. I start yelling, "No, no, no!" but she can't hear me, or she is completely ignoring me. I raise my palms, facing them toward her, trying to signal her to stop. My actions have no impact. She is even running faster as if there is no window in front of her. For a moment, I doubt whether she can stop in time and not crash into it. The doorbell keeps ringing, and she is almost at our beloved, iconic, king-sized, and very expensive, irreplaceable window. My wife walks over to the door, and I run toward the back door to deviate our dog from her path of destruction.

I am too late.

She leaps into the window, all four paws at the *same time*. The triple glass no longer feels that triple, emitting a deep, hollow sound. As she lands on her two back paws, she still has her front paws against the window, scratching with her nails as if desperately seeking, blindly, to find a door handle.

I finally open our back door, and she comes running into the house, determined to give our guests at the front door a proper and overenthusiastic crotch sniffle. It is an embarrassing scene that always makes me wonder why we didn't go for a smaller-sized dog when we had the chance. There is no way to hold her back. She is already strong and strong-headed.

Before I greet the guests, I quickly check the window for scratches. Knowing that it is impossible to replace it, I have been very concerned about scratches since the first moment our dog started jumping up on it. And yes, I see them – small, very thin scratches that were added this time or yesterday when she jumped up on the glass as well.

I have already been thinking about how I can keep the dog from jumping up on the window. I hate the idea of looking through a scratched window for the rest of our days in this house. This thought deeply concerns me. When my brother, the architect, designed the house, he added a pond next to this window, which we could see from the living room and kitchen. With a pond right there, the dog couldn't reach the window. We loved the idea but didn't immediately install it because of the costs. At this point, it is still a significant investment that we are not yet prepared to make. But it would be a great solution.

The sight of the extra scratches on the window irritates me no end. I need to manage myself as we have guests who deserve a proper warm welcome. The only thing that comes to mind, giving me a small measure of relief, is the idea that I will take a shovel when the guests leave and … (no, I am not going to kill the dog; this is not that kind of book) and start digging the pond myself. The investment has kept us from installing it up until this moment. But now, nothing's holding me back. I will just start digging myself, using my own hands and my own time, and I will figure it out as I go along. I have no idea how fishponds should be created, but that jump on the window led to a powerful inception, on the verge of obsession. No more scratches as of this moment forward.

Our guests leave later; it is still early evening. I look at my wife. She sees my expression and asks what's going on. I start grinning, probably looking a bit like a psychopath, and tell her, "Sweetie, I am going to dig a hole in the ground for our pond." She looks puzzled at first and then starts smiling. She thinks I am joking. I tell her again, "For real, do you know where the shovel is?"

She tells me it is in the garage where I left it and then asks, "But, are you going to dig a pond right now, at night?"

I respond, "Well, not the whole thing … but I will dig as deeply as necessary so our dog can't reach our window anymore whenever someone comes to the door." My own words sound magical to my ears. My wife calls me insane and says she's going to get the kids ready for bed. I'm feeling pretty great. So I grab the shovel, put on my boots and raincoat, and start digging outside next to the window.

After two hours of digging, I notice I haven't gotten very far, but just far enough to keep the dog from jumping up on the window. When I came up with my genius plan, completely on impulse, I neglected the fact that I needed to bring the excavated soil all the way around the house to a spot at the back of the garden, which I couldn't reach directly – due to a fence. This means that every time I filled the wheelbarrow with soil, I had to wheel it to the front of the house, around the house, and then all the way to the back over the road – about 40 meters each time.

In the first hour, it didn't bother me; I was full of adrenaline. During the second hour, it grew a bit painful. But I persisted until enough soil was dug out to create a large enough ditch. After two hours, I felt peaceful inside and hopeful about my plan. My wife looked at the ditch and me and responded with, "This is interesting," meaning she was in disbelief that I'd keep digging this hole myself.

What happened next was an unforgettable journey of despair and repair – one I'll bore my grandkids with until they get extremely sick of it. I spent a month digging a couple of hours almost every day. The shovel broke at one point; I fixed it with tie wraps and kept using it. The wheelbarrow wheel broke, too; I did a makeshift fix so I could still use it. A five-year-old tree with roots going deeper than I imagined was in the way. Initially, I planned to just dig out 4x3 meters, 1.5 meters deep. But halfway through, I realized I had to add 2x3 meters because I needed space for the pumps and filters.

Obstacles like broken tools, rocks, the tree, and incessant pouring rain worked against me. I don't think it ever rained as much as it did that month. My desk-job hands got blisters quickly, but I powered through. Everything hurt during – and after – shoveling.

But seeing progress made me dream of the beautiful future pond – I could see it clearly, motivating me onward. The hole grew bigger. My impressed kids and wife doubled my motivation. I'd see them watching a movie through the window as I toiled rain-soaked in mud, feeling good about myself. My sons would give me a quick glance through the window, giving me a quick thumbs up.

My friends told me to rent a Bobcat Backhoe instead of breaking my back. But I couldn't – this felt personal, like I had to dig it myself, overcoming odds with my bare hands without help. I would see the hole in the ground growing bigger and bigger. It called me every day. And I got back out there and shoveled until my body told me to stop. When it was finally finished, I didn't want to lose that feeling of building something with my own hands and seeing it come to life, even if it was just a muddy hole in the ground.

To me, it was already a fishpond in my mind. I ended up digging out more than I had to, extending completion by having to refill parts. When truly done with the hole, I felt immensely satisfied. Our dog watched the whole process, sometimes accidentally pushing dirt back in – surely thinking, "There are other windows; are you digging holes for all of them?"

Collective understanding will fade if thinking doesn't shift to doing.

I felt like giving up a few times. It was painful, but I couldn't quit. I became so obsessed with getting that hole that I often worked until late at night. The idea of the scratched window and the vision of having a beautiful pond we could see from our kitchen and living room kept me going. Encouragement from my family along the way, seeing the tangible results and progress, and having all the tools on hand to start any time I wanted helped me stick with it until it was done.

That moment when I had a very clear vision of what I wanted, and the dog gave the final push to make it happen – that was the spark. It was so strong, continually pulling me back to the work. I call that kind of charged moment "inception" – the start of something new, a conviction that hooks us into action. The source of grit and perseverance. The drive that refocuses us again and again to bring something into reality. That inception gets us to turn thinking into actual doing, into reality.

Inception is the final tenet of making space. If it happens at the end of a co-creative moment, it is the start of making space to materialize the outcome of the co-creation.

I finished the pond at a very reasonable price. It wouldn't exist if I had gotten stuck thinking about all the reasons we shouldn't invest in the pond. It is there because I just started "doing." I enjoy looking out at our pond every day. It symbolizes strength and focus to me. It reminds me that all you need to do is start *acting* when you want to bring something to life.

THE ULTIMATE ANCHOR
Every creation starts as an idea that becomes conceptualized into a tangible form. It is then brought to life through a process of implementation. Acting upon it repetitively integrates it into our reality.

This happens on both micro and macro levels. When we learn something new, our initial thinking creates new neural wiring. Practicing or acting upon it regularly provides emotional experiences through our body's involvement. Over time, it becomes a habit or feels normal.

Similarly, on a macro level, a way of thinking can influence collective thought. A shared mindset leads to certain behaviors growing among a community, organization, or population as they implement ideas. Eventually, it evolves into an embedded culture where people share a way of doing things that aligns with their collective mindset without consciously thinking about it.

A co-creative session that comes into existence by making space – using the switch, the hook, depatterning, and anchoring – plants the seeds for a new collective mindset. It is the time in space when all participants belong to the moment they have experienced. This moment results in a new way of seeing things, new possibilities, new beliefs, and a new understanding. That was what the space was made for: to allow for this new collective understanding.

However, this collective understanding will fade if thinking doesn't shift to doing. The new neural wiring will be pruned again if it isn't fueled with experiences that further shape and fuel the mindset. Therefore, if doing doesn't happen, the space might as well never have been created. A faint memory that will fade away. An addition to the graveyard of workshops that never led to anything.

"Inception" is about expanding space to generate action. I like to call this the *ultimate anchor*, as it should dig deep into the minds and intentions of the participants. This final anchoring is the start of the movement required to drive change.

You can think about how to drive a car, but you won't become an experienced driver if you don't invest energy in getting your license, getting a car, and practicing driving around. Inception is when you plan to take steps, the moment you start strategizing how to make it happen. Where can I get my license? What is necessary to attain it? What are my obstacles, and how can I overcome them?

Inception is making space to turn intentions into reality – the most common challenge when innovating how you do things. It's getting an idea off the drawing board while facing all the obstacles working against realizing your vision. It requires an ultimate "anchor" to keep pulling your attention back into the process of realization, competing against other projects on your radar and daily distractions.

OWNERSHIP
As with everything created in life, momentum is required for things to start flowing. At this stage, at the end of a co-creative moment, the outcome is still just a concept, far from material. It is volatile and can easily evaporate.

As Rick Rubin explains in his book, *The Creative Act: A Way of Being*, any idea is channeled from the creative field – if you don't act on it, someone else will. It is bound to materialize somehow. This inception moment is crucial for kicking off the ownership of materializing what is still conceptual.

A group must move the outcome from an abstract idea to concrete next steps. This movement and tangible planning prevent a vision from remaining nebulous and unsupported. *Acting* on the creative spark brings it to life.

Whether the participants can build momentum and drive change depends on their grit and audacity. The more strongly they believe in and take ownership of the outcome, the more influential their thought field becomes – both individually and collectively (in terms of energy psychology). As they act on their beliefs with the necessary focus and adaptability, their thought fields will influence others and scale change.

You can think of it as the influence a charismatic, strong-minded leader has in creating a movement and expanding a collective mindset. That level of influence stems from their unwavering focus and belief. In terms of energy psychology, it is a robust thought field that substantially sways how others think.

Similar to how some people might be "super-spreaders" of a virus, certain individuals can be very influential with strong beliefs. If a collective group does not feel a strong sense of ownership over an outcome and the desire to bring it to life, their combined energy will fail to generate momentum. There will be little space created for new realities to manifest. For a vision to materialize, participants must become "super-spreaders" of the ideas – deeply believing in and committed to realizing the outcome.

Inception, the ultimate anchor, aims to consciously build the necessary ownership. This ownership is the ingraining of the "pull" that keeps drawing their attention back for multiple moments of materializing. Each moment space is made to act upon a vision, and inception is strengthened.

INCEPTION IS STRATEGY
The hook plays a vital role in generating the motivation to turn intentions into strategy during inception. But motivation isn't enough to move forward. You have to step on the gas and overcome obstacles on your way. That is strategy! Inception is strategizing and re-strategizing to bring the concept, the outcome of the moment, to life.

In his best-selling books, including *Unlimited Power* and *Awaken the Giant Within*, Tony Robbins often emphasizes that individuals must learn to consciously leverage the power of pain and pleasure to create meaningful change and achieve success. Rather than allowing fear of pain to hold them back or seeking short-term pleasure at the expense of long-term goals, he encourages people to reframe their mindsets. This involves associating more pleasure with taking positive actions and achieving goals while also recognizing the pain of remaining stagnant or not pursuing one's aspirations.

His words make a strong case for generating the necessary strategy and energy among participants during inception, including helping them associate positive returns with their planned actions and imagining negative outcomes for not taking action. Building a strategy to turn intentions into reality is not only an exercise of the rational mind; it should always include stirring up emotions that motivate action.

A few key things need to emerge from that final inception phase to drive motivated momentum:

- Everyone should be able to imagine small successes from the initial actions they define.
- Measurements are needed, ideally qualitative, emotion-based measures rather than quantitative KPIs, to provide a sense of progress.
- Everyone involved needs to connect to build a feeling of community and have a platform that supports channeling positive affirmations to each other. Positive affirmations generate dopamine, the motivational neurotransmitter that fuels behavior.
- Stress needs to be properly managed. It corrodes the hooks and takes away all motivation. Resilience and stress management skills are essential to driving change constructively. Without them, affirmations are ineffective.
- A collaboration routine should be established or kickstarted, e.g., regular touchpoints, information-sharing habits, constructive meeting versus workshop approach, planned days of focus work on the project, etc. These are elements that need to be addressed during inception.

In summary, participants must be able to visualize success, track progress emotionally, connect as a community, manage stress, and develop a habit of working together. Meeting these needs during inception powers motivation to realize the vision. Inception is making space to make space.

FROM THINKING TO DOING

Inception is the start of turning the thinking from the co-creative moment into the doing. As described before, it takes motivation and strategy. Although it seems very obvious, this is the part where most people struggle. With everything they need to manage and all the goals they need to achieve, it is hard to turn anything additional into another list of action points and prioritize them to act upon. Knowing this, we have to make the inception part as straightforward as possible. We can translate the key things that drive motivated momentum, explained in the previous part, into a simple three-step strategy with the help of BJ Fogg's MAP Model from *Tiny Habits*. In his MAP framework, BJ Fogg explains the three most important aspects of behavior change: motivation, ability, and prompting. An even more concise and powerful version of those same key things:

MOTIVATION. People need to be motivated to act; they need their hook as well as the positive return from taking action, the tangible effect, and positive affirmations.
The scratches on my window. The admiration of my family. Seeing the hole growing bigger.

ABILITY. They also need to feel able to take the required action; it needs to fit their capabilities, and they need to have the time to pay some focused attention.
The shovel and wheelbarrow at hand. The hours in the evening at home. Physical strength.

PROMPTING. Finally, they need reminders and some routine prompting them to act at the right time and place.
Seeing the work and potential end result right outside my window every day.

Many frameworks have been developed to summarize what people need to exhibit behavior that manifests new realities. In addition to Tony Robbins' theories and BJ Fogg's MAP Model are the Transtheoretical Model, Social Cognitive Theory, and the Theory of Planned Behavior. All of these emphasize similar key factors: willingness/motivation, ability/capability, structure/opportunity, and learning/progress. BJ Fogg's MAP Model is one of the most practical ones to build upon.

To make this as simple as possible, these are the three things we need to figure out to achieve a strong inception, a strong anchor for our attention to keep taking action:

- How strong is my "pull" to sufficiently direct my attention to the necessary tasks?
- How capable do I feel of making it happen?
- How organized am I to maintain and even increase momentum?

From working with talented people across organizations, I believe almost all of them feel capable, or at least surround themselves with the right capabilities, to do the tasks needed to bring concepts into reality.

Their personal work ethic, experience, resourcefulness, and the tools and support they have in their organizations lead me to believe that most people can also organize themselves to get momentum in their actions. Incremental progress.

What I often see lacking is the strong "pull" of their attention to overcome obstacles and persevere to achieve their goals. The initial hook answers "In what way can this matter to me?" The outcomes of the co-creative moment will likely have some personal returns related to that initial hook.

For example, if you were fully in the moment because you longed for some recognition and support for your work on a project, you just might have had some of that during the shared moment. But that initial hook into the moment might not be enough to provide the lasting motivation you need to act. Getting recognition and support might not be sufficient to keep your attention on achieving bigger goals over time. You need a twist on your hook. That twist should allow for a clear positive return and positive peer affirmations.

THE HOOK TWIST
To get yourself hooked into a co-creative moment, keeping your attention on it, making space for the moment to happen, you answered "In what way can this matter to me?" Now that the moment is closing with the inception, you have to become hooked on the future moments that need your attention to take action. You are making space to prepare for making space in the future. The question you need to answer becomes, "In what way can *I* matter to make this happen?"

The "pull" of your hook twist will determine the strength of the inception. The same logic applies as with the initial hook. It is a personal investigation to understand how you can matter to help bring the outcome of the moment to life. But it will be ten times stronger if everyone shares and bonds over their hook twists. It is the source of positive feedback and acknowledgments toward each other.

I explained earlier in this book how Design Thinking is questioned. The real reason for this questioning is that organizations are not creating a culture that allows enough space for Design Thinking to flourish. If people in organizations co-create to bring new realities to life, whether they call it Design Thinking or any other name, they need to make space for it. Managing innovation with strict, emotionless KPIs and a culture of stress and pressure creates more of the same because there is no space for the unknown to become new realities. Fear leads to a lack of daring – a lack of daring to take chances, be vulnerable, make mistakes, and open up to new ways of looking at things. This results in repeating the same old patterns. In this kind of culture, the inception, which is the culminating co-creative moment, is not properly handled with care. There is no ultimate anchor created for all participants to make space for action. They aren't equipped with a strong "attention grabber" that needs to last long enough to drive change when change is resisted and distractions are everywhere.

The strength of this inception is the hook (why *it* matters to you) and the twisted hook (why *you* matter to it) that arises from the co-created moment.

Answering the question, "In what way can I matter to help move this forward?" calls upon your understanding of your skills, personality, and experience. Knowing what you can contribute (why you matter) is the strongest hook there is. Stepping into your power is what inception is all about. It leads to potentially getting positive affirmations and acknowledgments from your peers, which is a powerful confirmation of why you matter.

Organizations don't have strong inceptions at the end of co-creative moments because they don't help their people discover the kind of contributions they can make. They don't help their people step into their power enough. Some organizational cultures even rob their people of their power, making them feel small and expendable. Undoubtedly, thriving organizations are filled with people who know their strengths and have no problem finding their hook twists – understanding their important role in making things happen. This is the strongest motivation to make space. This is the essence of the ultimate hook. If you know how you matter, you will always make space to chase that feeling of mattering.

Let's investigate what practices can help us achieve a strong inception at the end of a co-creative moment.

INCEPTION
Experiments

PERSONAL AND GROUP EXPERIMENTS

This practice aims to help you take on the responsibility of achieving a strong inception for yourself at the end of shared moments. It should help you build your ownership and make you more effective and productive – in other words, more in tune with your capabilities.

This moment of inception is the ultimate anchor and can only happen as a group. Hence, this practical part is written as a combination of personal and group practices that happen simultaneously. The personal practices only have value within the context of a group practice.

MY PERSONAL PRACTICE
At the end of each shared moment, I ask myself what the inception should be like. What is it that deserves our attention when the moment is over? There is always at least one thing that needs to be acted upon. Usually, there are a couple of things. I tend to initiate the summary of the outcome, particularly the elements that need some action, but I also provide space for anyone who spontaneously starts summarizing. It is important to me that everyone is clear on the actionable items before I start suggesting things I can do.

When all is clear and agreed upon, I start by suggesting action points that I love doing, which have an impact, and that get me excited because I can learn something or experience something new. Those are the ones I put forward first because I know it will be easy to stay motivated to do something about it. Second, I would suggest action points that I know I am in a unique or best position to get done. These might not be to-dos that I particularly like doing, but they are the ones that give me a good sense of contribution.

While thinking about and sharing the contribution I can make to the common cause, the obstacles would have already crossed my mind. I try to make it easy on myself to make things happen, so I would ask all the others whether they have an idea about how to deal with the forces that work against me. I would only think about the obstacles I know I won't be able to solve myself or the ones where I know others are perfectly placed to help me. For example, I would ask if anyone could introduce me to the key person I need to talk with or if anyone knows who is responsible for the process related to my task, etc.

I am a big fan of prompt shots (explained in the next part). I would be the one setting these up, and I would ask someone else to be an Archiver, helping with the organization of any material we gather in one spot. I am not a good Archiver and would probably mess it up for everyone.

I always ensure everyone is involved in the conversations about each participant's contributions, helping each other with obstacles, and organizing some prompting and practical things. I pay close attention to whether I feel there is co-ownership being built. If I am not feeling it, I show some appreciation for the commitments everyone is making and emphasize how great it would be to achieve our vision or goals. That type of acknowledgment fuels pride and ownership. I would also be the first to start giving positive feedback when others are doing their part, making sure it is visible and authentic so that, hopefully, the others will start doing the same kind of positive affirmations as we take on our to-dos. They always do.

In a workshop, as a facilitator, I allocate a significant amount of time for inception. Without building ownership and making space to ensure everyone makes space for the "doing," the workshop has no value.

BOUNDARIES

If everyone in the team explores how they can matter in order to make things happen, boundaries of ownership are generated naturally and easily agreed upon. Understanding where your contributions end and others' contributions begin comes naturally if everyone takes ownership.

Everyone taking ownership is probably not always the default case. If you are one of the few who understands the importance of inception at the end of a shared moment, you might end up with an overload of tasks to do. If that is the risk of your shared moment with others, you have to make use of the inception to build ownership. The inception is a three-step strategy to help you and others create a sense of ownership. But if that isn't enough, agreeing on "roles for action" in the group can also help, as explained below.

FINAL ANCHORING TO PROGRESS

Before any inception can occur, everyone has to become very clear on what the outcome of the shared moment is and what it is everyone wants to bring to life.

The initial hook is very important to become motivated to strategize around taking action. Therefore, it is important to have a final "anchoring to progress" moment with the group, outlining the most important conclusions of the shared moment while everyone relates it to their personal hook.

Inception starts when all individuals reflect on what came out of the shared moment and in what way it matters to them personally. The combination of what came out within the context of what matters will help identify what should be taken further into action. If everyone takes such a moment to interpret all that has been said and creates a short list of the things that the group should make happen in the immediate and longer terms, everyone gets brought into the inception. Everyone has a stake.

This can feel like an awkward and cumbersome collective practice at the end of a quick meeting. You don't have to roll this out in an elaborate way when it doesn't suit the moment. It can be as simple as suggesting to your fellow co-creators, "Hey, let's take a quick moment together to list what we all find important to work on after this meeting. Where has this meeting brought us together?" and take a pen to write things down for everyone.

In a workshop setting, the outcomes can become more complicated and bigger, so a good amount of time for people to work in silence on their interpretation of valuable pursuits for the team makes sense. If everyone shares their thoughts one by one, starting with, "What really matters to me … (hook)", followed by "Which is why I feel we need to focus on …(goals)", the group ends up with a concise list of things that need to be achieved. If it is a mix of short-term and long-term goals, they can be categorized into different horizons by the group: things they need to act on immediately; things they need to plan; and things they need to investigate.

The shared hooks are at least as important as the goals. Particularly if multiple people in the workshop have similar reasons why the goals matter to them; this can lead to strong bonding and co-ownership. It would be a mistake to emphasize the goals more than the hooks because the goals wouldn't have come into existence if it weren't for the hooks. A common mistake is to rush the start of the inception and efface any emotion to line the goals up rationally. Emotions get people to feel ownership, not the goals themselves.

If every participant in a shared moment is clear on what deserves attention to be brought to life and, especially, why, inception has begun.

MOTIVATION
How strong is my "pull" to direct my attention sufficiently to the necessary tasks?

Inception is strategy. Step 1 is to ensure everyone assesses the strength of the "pull" for their attention. When outlining the goals, everyone knows why they should make things happen. The next step is to think about "in what way can I matter to achieve them."

This part cannot be imposed on anyone. If tasks are distributed without people suggesting how they would like to contribute, there is usually no real ownership. It is not because someone gets paid or receives "carrots" to carry out tasks that they will feel intrinsically motivated to carry them out. Without intrinsic motivation, they will get easily distracted and come up with all kinds of reasons why they can't make space for action. Or they might make fake space, pretending they invested their talents and energy but just did a quick fix, leading to less-than-optimal qualitative results.

Every participant in a shared moment should be given the opportunity to suggest their own "hook twist." Whatever they feel they can contribute is also what they will potentially have appreciation for. Having everyone share the actions they want to take is a great way to create a solid support base to give each other acknowledgments and positive affirmations. Basically, if everyone knows what the other wants to be doing, it becomes easy to rely on each other and become appreciative of their efforts. Positive returns and positive affirmations are part of all the behavioral frameworks I have encountered. Besides installing KPIs, there should always be a good support base installed to give each other appraisals and signs of appreciation.

Whatever contributions participants suggest will also evolve over time as there are multiple shared moments related to a project and multiple moments of inception. With positive affirmations about their efforts, people will suggest more significant commitments during the next inceptions, feeling supported by the group.

Therefore, none of the contributions anyone suggests should be judged or critiqued. Allowing everyone to find their own role in carrying out the next steps is crucial for cultivating ownership.

The hook twist and the potential for positive feedback on one's efforts are the most important strategic elements of inception. Inception is a strategy to get things done. Inception is ownership by all involved. Therefore, inception is about creating a mechanism for each individual to seek the pleasure of recognition and avoid the pain of shame.

When inception becomes a familiar concept, and everyone consciously takes time for it at the end of each co-creative moment, the hook twist is a great opportunity to be recognized by one's peers. And that is exactly what it should feel like. At the end of each co-creative moment, participants should be excited to show their capabilities and contributions, knowing they will be appreciated for it. No money in the world can replace genuine appreciation by one's peers. An artist can become a millionaire, but if their peers consider their next piece of art useless rubbish, they feel a loss of identity and emptiness. Peer recognition in a valued community gives people drive.

It takes only one person to lead by example and show appreciation to get others to do the same. By making this appreciative behavior visible and creating platforms for it, it can more easily become a part of the culture.

ABILITY
How capable do I feel of making it happen?

By now, all the participants know what to achieve and why, and they know what they want to do themselves. The next step would be to think about the obstacles. These are the things you need to figure out or the group needs to help you overcome. If these obstacles are a given and can't be solved or avoided, the whole group needs to acknowledge them and see the difficulty. This step prevents the participants from losing their feeling of ownership when confronted with the first big obstacle.

In a workshop setting, it would be considered normal to take the time to investigate forces that work against certain actions and then discuss any good strategies to avoid or overcome them with the group. These obstacles can be categorized by the group as: "avoided by …", "overcome with …" and "on our radar for future strategizing." The last column of "unavoidable obstacles" is the one everyone agrees to not become intimidated or discouraged by. It is the reality the whole group accepts to work in and trusts it will be handled when the time is right.

In a meeting, this would happen more on the fly. After summarizing some things that might be interesting to bring to life, one person can immediately suggest what they see as their next step, followed by the others doing the same. When shared and agreed upon, the "deal" can be closed by asking each other what they need help with or if anything can make their lives easier. If any, the meeting participants can provide their support or services to help each other with whatever they committed to doing.

I'm sure many people take care of a moment of inception at the end of every meeting. I am also sure these are very effective people that get a lot done.

I am not so sure if *everyone* intentionally has a proper moment of inception at the end of their meetings. If space isn't made for inception, participants won't have any ownership, and nothing will materialize. No inception lowers the meeting back to collaboration from co-creation despite the switch, hook, depatterning, and anchoring. This last inception part should be considered consciously by everyone at the end of any shared moment, big or small.

PROMPTING
How organized am I to maintain and even increase momentum?

Even if we are motivated, supported by our peers, and feel capable despite the obstacles, a structure still needs to be put in place to help with taking action. We need to be reminded to take action and stay connected with others when taking action.

In a workshop setting, this final Step 3 of inception should become a group exercise to decide how to work. When is our next gathering? Where do we share the results of our actions or resources? What kind of prompting can we put in place to remind everyone to act? What kind of timing are we working with? As with the previous steps, it would be a combination of personally figuring out how much time is required, how everyone wants to communicate on progress, and where to find some tools or resources to help. Group consolidation is needed on how this personal approach can come together in one collaborative approach that works for everyone.

In a workshop, it can become an activity dedicated to outlining the "how" to take action. In a small meeting, there wouldn't be as much space to dig into the how. A common practice in a small meeting would be to agree upon the next time to reconvene to share and assess progress. What is not so common and very effective is helping each other install prompts and reminders to take action. This is specifically important for meetings. A workshop usually has a significant impact in and of itself and is likely to result in a structured approach. In a meeting, you don't typically dive into setting up a structured approach for next steps. And therefore, agreeing on small reminders to make space for it can be very helpful.

These days, people often set up temporary Teams Chat or WhatsApp groups to have a channel for prompting and messaging each other. But that can also add to the clutter of messages you receive daily, cluttering the space you make for other things.

Another great way to help each other with reminding, or prompting, is to set up the next touchpoint in the calendar, but only making it 10 minutes – 10 minutes of check-in. You can combine it with a coffee or tea moment if you are present in the same office, or it could be a quick online touchpoint. Because it is only 10 minutes and meant to be a prompt, you have to be disciplined and stick to prompting.

To prepare for this moment you can ask each other what kind of prompts you each might need. Which topics or items do you want to be reminded of? And those are the ones you quickly share with each other. The prompt touchpoint can end with a specific request for an extra meeting or a file to be sent, but it shouldn't turn into a longer conversation. Prompting touchpoints are great for keeping that connection and getting reminded without cluttering your day with distractive messages or adding more workload with extra meetings. I like to call them "Prompt Shots".

ROLES FOR ACTION

If the inception doesn't lead to an equal distribution of ownership among the group members, it can help to agree upon some roles people will take on to help everyone make it happen. These are supporting roles to enable everyone to do their own tasks. Such roles add more momentum to the "doing." I have effectively worked with agreeing upon three extra roles on top of the agreed contributions everyone will commit to: the Chaser, the Archiver, and the Organizer. These roles would usually be taken on by people who didn't figure out how they could contribute or have difficulty finding their way to making it happen. These roles still give them a sense of ownership.

THE CHASER

This person takes on the duty of prompting team members to take action on their assigned tasks. The Chaser agrees on the most appropriate or convenient communication channels with the team to prompt them. Via these channels, the Chaser will remind each team member of the tasks, timing, and any other updates regarding their tasks, like the availability of information stored in the team's archive.

The Chaser keeps track of all the tasks and who is performing them. This makes the Chaser a perfect point of contact if anyone needs to know the status of a task being completed by another team member.

THE ARCHIVER

The Archiver is the team member who agrees to organize all the gathered materials necessary to execute. The Archiver notifies the Chaser if anything gets added to the archive so that the Chaser can update specific team members on the availability of information. The Archiver might have conveniently taken on the tasks to gather certain information, or they might receive information from team members to store in the team's archive.

As the Chaser agrees with the team on which channels to use for prompting, the Archiver agrees with the team on which platform to archive the materials.

If you don't have an Archiver assigned and team members add documents and other types of information on a platform by themselves, it might become messy, and the team members who need the information might not be informed of the availability. The Archiver removes the hurdle of not having (or being able to find) the right information.

THE ORGANIZER

The Organizer arranges the team meetings, such as the next time to reconvene the team whenever the team is close to ending the first stage. The Organizer doesn't organize any specific meetings related to specific tasks of a team member. Instead, they will ensure that the team connects at the right time with available team members.
Just as the Chaser agrees on channels and the Archiver agrees on the platform, the Organizer agrees on the timing and frequency of team meetings with all team members.

This can become part of an activity in a workshop where you agree with the group on how to work. However, it can also be applied to meetings in a smaller and more straightforward format. There could be a support function briefed to chase, organize, and archive. Or the participants of the shared moment can agree upon someone who receives all resources from everyone to make them available in one spot and someone who sets up some prompt shots and finds space in everyone's calendar for the next gathering.

Dear Diary,

I am at peace with the concept of purpose in my life. The retreat opened my eyes to a different way of thinking about purpose. I often ask myself in what way a shared moment can matter to me. I find personal meaning and a great reason to keep my attention in that moment. It makes every moment meaningful. All those reasons why shared moments matter to me show a red thread, revealing what I long for in my life. Meaning is not one clear purpose; meaning evolves along with me and the phases in my life. Although I love this newfound perspective on purpose, there was still something missing. Finding meaning in shared moments doesn't help with actualizing myself; it only brings a passive understanding of what is important to me. Self-actualization is my embodiment of meaning. I know. It is deep. Maybe too deep. I feel uncomfortable playing around with such intangible philosophical concepts. Bear with me, Diary. Almost there. I discovered that by twisting this question at the end of a shared moment into, "In what way can I matter to this outcome?" not only did the shared moment matter more to me, but the outcome now matters to me. And I am becoming part of it by acting upon it in a meaningful way. Applying my talents, strengths or unique capabilities to bring it to life. Like I said, I am at peace. This makes me less restless. I now understand that each shared moment in itself is something to cherish. Even seemingly unimportant encounters can matter, and whatever comes out can activate me in a meaningful way, giving me a sense of contribution. "In what way can this matter to me?" and "How can I matter to the outcome?" are both reflections that help me step off the hamster wheel. Simply because I am not chasing some big achievement to find meaning, I find more than enough meaning in everyday moments. I should write a book about this. Everyone should feel the way I feel. There is no reason to chase things; everything is already here if you pay attention.

Your Vaganaut

PART 3
Unlock Collective Genius

CHAPTER 8. MAKING SPACE IN MEETINGS AND WORKSHOPS

"I didn't know you could design a thought process for a workshop. In our team, when something requires our attention, we sit in a meeting room and discuss it for an hour or two. These meetings are always the same. We have an agenda, and we cover each point one by one. Our manager usually takes the lead. The same people are always vocal about their opinions. The conversations become circular, and the outcomes feel predetermined. We always have these discussions with the same team. For example, we rarely invite others to join if we have something that needs solving. Learning about designing for certain conversations to happen in a thought-through sequence to get to more controversy, deeper understanding, and eventually, better outcomes is like a revelation to me."

This feedback from my facilitation training doesn't really come as a surprise. I've listened to many people describe similar meeting cultures. I've also had numerous conversations with course participants about the difference between meetings and workshops and when one format is more appropriate.

Design-driven organizations, consultancies, and companies in creative industries are all familiar with the concept of workshops, although not all of them run good ones. Organizations in more traditional industries like finance, manufacturing, energy, transport, and heavy industry are more familiar with meetings but not so much with workshops.

Conversations with my course participants made it clear that there's often confusion about when to have a meeting and when to "workshop it." Complicated topics that generate a lot of opinions are frequently tackled in open table conversations instead of a structured workshop with good facilitation. These conversations obviously go everywhere and nowhere, resulting in little actionability and very little ownership. Some topics are just too complicated to tackle with an unguided conversation.

Some topics are just too complicated to tackle with an unguided conversation.

MEETINGS VS. WORKSHOPS

Understanding collectively when to have a meeting and when to have a workshop can already greatly improve a group's meeting culture.

What is the difference, and when is one more appropriate than the other?

As the words already imply:

- A **meeting** is a planned moment where people come together to have open-ended discussions about topics that require their attention, allowing the conversation to flow spontaneously.
- A **workshop** is a planned moment where participants work on topics in a structured manner to achieve outcomes, leveraging the collective knowledge and genius of everyone present to the fullest extent possible.

Workshops can unlock and accelerate projects. Meetings can keep things going.

The big difference between a meeting and a workshop is that conversations in meetings happen impromptu. In contrast, conversations in workshops are triggered by a meticulously designed flow of activities.

When might an impromptu table discussion not lead to the best possible results, with buy-in from all involved? Well, when:

- Topics have a host of different interpretations.
- Stakeholders have very different stakes.
- Solutions are not obvious.
- A topic or challenge sparks a good amount of controversy.
- The outcomes are pivotal.

Meetings are good for topics needing spontaneous reflection to move forward. Workshops are necessary when specific thought processes need to be triggered in a sequence that allows for breakthrough moments. Workshops can unlock and accelerate projects. Meetings can keep things going.

Having one workshop about a difficult topic can save you ten inefficient meetings about it. On the other hand, having workshops for every little thing that needs to be discussed is overkill and a waste of time. Knowing how to balance meetings against workshops is a sign of a healthy meeting culture.

REQUIREMENTS FOR AN EFFECTIVE MEETING CULTURE

Knowing how to balance meetings against workshops is like having only one shoe tied to win a race. All participants also need to know how to make space to have an effective meeting culture. Strategically balancing meetings with workshops and having a collective ability to make space for shared moments brings out an organization's collective genius.

Striking the right balance between meetings and workshops is crucial to effectively arrive at the best outcomes together. Making space for a meeting or workshop elevates the moment from mere collaboration to co-creation. The depth of the space determines the quality of the outcome.

Making space in meetings versus workshops is very similar. Both types of gatherings require all 5 tenets. The switch, the hook, and anchoring can happen individually, but sharing them can also add value in meetings and workshops alike. The inception might be a bit more elaborate in a workshop, having more output that requires a stronger sense of co-ownership than meetings. In other words, the implementation afterward will probably be more complicated and extensive. So, more strategizing is needed to make it happen. Of the 5 tenets, there is only one that is applied very differently between meetings and workshops: depatterning.

As conversations in meetings happen impromptu and usually aim to keep workstreams moving forward, there is no need to break the thinking and behavioral patterns that much. The level of co-creation required in meetings only extends to understanding the current situation from different perspectives and determining the desired near-future direction.

Conversations in workshops are deliberately triggered to discover new possibilities to explore. It requires the participants to break their thinking and behavioral patterns and see things differently. Because the topics are more complicated to tackle, there is more uncertainty about the outcome of the gathering and more risk involved in arriving at an outcome that doesn't deliver the desired progress. The level of co-creation goes deeper compared to meetings. Hence, they take more time and effort. People with specific expertise are invited, tools and activities are designed for controversy, and the conversations are facilitated to arrive at valuable new insights. Everything is intentionally put in place to depattern and unlock the collective genius as much as possible.

DEPATTERNING IN MEETINGS VS WORKSHOPS

In meetings, depatterning is basically active listening. By making sure you hold the space for everyone to share their thoughts and listen with curiosity to gain a broader understanding, you are making space for the best outcomes. It will also be a lot easier to observe your own thoughts while actively listening to others compared to when you are spending most of the time making your points. When you explain and try to convince others of your opinions, you become your opinions, leaving little room for other perspectives. Paying attention to holding the space at least as much as filling the space, combined with short moments of silence to reflect, leads to sufficient depatterning in meetings for better outcomes.

In workshops, depatterning is an art. A good facilitator will always look for tools, techniques, and settings that allow the unknown to emerge. At the end of Chapter 5, we covered a couple of tactics that can be applied for a depatterning effect. This makes a tremendous difference in the quality of the outcomes of workshops.

Many organizations seek methodologies to help them become more innovative. But all that organizations really need to be innovative are two things:

1. A good facilitator who can be creative in how they design the depatterning, keeping in mind the audience and the required outcomes at a given project stage.
2. People who've become more aware of their patterns and seek depatterning when co-creating in a workshop. In other words, participants who are proficient at applying the 5 tenets to make space.

Participants who have less resistance when navigating the facilitator's depatterning activities and who apply the necessary cognitive flexibility achieve amazing co-creative results.

In my previous book, *Captains of Leadership: Build your Facilitative Confidence*, the reader is invited to grow as a facilitator, developing skills to help workshop participants consider new perspectives and co-create from the unknown. From years of applying these facilitation skills myself, I have noticed that having a good facilitator who masters these techniques is not enough on its own to achieve the best possible outcomes. Participants also need to know how to make space, become aware of their personal patterns, and be willing to depattern. Particularly in this age of distraction, it seems very hard for participants to keep their attention in the moment and maintain a relaxed, co-creative state, allowing them to see things differently. Having lost the ability to switch, find their hook, and anchor their attention, their level of attention is compromised. The space they make is not deep enough.

COLLECTIVE GENIUS

The strength of an organization lies in its collective genius. What an organization can achieve is determined by the sum of its parts, not by the individuals. You can recruit amazingly talented people who have achieved incredible things in their careers but can't seem to live up to expectations in your organization.

One person alone can't make the necessary difference; you have to unlock collective genius, the synergy that sparks from mixing people in a moment. That spark, the unlocking of collective genius, happens when collaboration in a given moment is elevated to co-creation.

The only way to unlock collective genius is to nurture a culture of making space. If all individuals learn how to apply the 5 tenets of making space during their meetings and workshops, facilitators will be able to bring out groundbreaking and disruptive magic.

It would be a mistake to rely only on methodologies. Collective genius is not unlocked by applying methodologies. I have painstakingly taught and applied methods like Design Thinking and Agile at organizations that didn't nurture a culture of making space. It didn't go anywhere, and it didn't have any significant results. Never trust the process if there isn't any space made by the participants. And if there is, design the process again and again to leverage that space and create moments that bring out collective genius.

> *Never trust the process if there isn't any space made by the participants.*

At its essence, an organization is a system that harnesses the collective intelligence of its people. Ironically, our ways of exchanging information in our organizational systems have become very sophisticated, but instead of bringing out our collective genius, they hamper it by leaving little space for it to emerge. Emails, chats, social channels, podcasts, and other outside-in personal channels keep us distracted in the shared moments that could provide the opportunity for collective intelligence to come into play.

Organizations that thrive on their collective intelligence are the ones with people who make space during meetings and workshops. Those gatherings are the key moments that can make all the difference.

CULTURE FOR MAKING SPACE

Making space at work brings out the collective genius of an organization. Realizing this value helps organizations decide to invest efforts in building a culture that makes space. Building such a culture requires, first and foremost, an increased awareness of the value of making space for shared moments. It also requires a language that brings the concept of "making space" to life in people's minds. Every culture exists because of a language that supports the collective thinking and behavior within that culture. Upon investigation, you'll notice that every culture and subculture has its own language. The way people communicate and the words they use to refer to certain cognitive concepts reflect their beliefs and drive their behavior. Without a language for making space, you cannot build a culture for it.

If I had to sum up why I wrote this book in one sentence, it is because I think there is still an incredible need within organizations to develop a language for "making space." There is a need for a language that will help raise even greater awareness and build the right culture for it.

I hope concepts like the switch, finding your hook, depatterning, anchoring your attention, and always looking out for a good inception become part of the organizational lingo, giving "making space" some social equity.

An organization with people making space, managing their mindsets, and paying attention to the point of inception leads to more shared ownership and less control. A strong sense of shared ownership among people in an organization allows for evolved constellations of the organizational system.

The 5 tenets are valuable not only in a work environment. Applying the 5 tenets to consciously make space also provides great insight into how you can better design your life.

Making space is a simple but powerful concept that makes you more conscious about sustaining your focus and directing your sustained focus, which impacts how you experience your life.

The next chapter sheds light on how consciously making space can change the way you live.

Dear Diary,

More was added to my plate ... but it is totally fine. I love this new responsibility I have been given. This past month, I have been raving to everyone about my new way of approaching the moments I share with other people in my work life and private life. I have been telling them about meaning, breaking patterns for creativity, and powerful attention. And I have been selling these concepts to them as a way of improving how we spend time together. I have been nudging them to consider these approaches so we can get the best out of our time spent together. There is a genius hiding somewhere in that moment when we share ideas and perspectives. My raving and nudging clearly caught everyone's attention. Management wants me to lead a project with HR that should improve our meeting culture. They seem to have lost their enthusiasm for big campaigns around company values and purpose. Instead, they seem to long for a culture where everyone is "making space" for creativity and co-creation. How about that! And they want to put me in the lead?! Dreamjob alert! I still have to figure out how I will get this one going, but I am already thinking about creating some easy principles to help people assess their level of attention and their intention when meeting. Maybe inspire some of them to become ambassadors to help create and use a language for these principles, to help turn them into topics of conversation. I also need to make sure people stop falling into the trap of trying to solve everything with open discussions. We need to build the competence of designing and leading structured gatherings to tackle our challenges, helping everyone manage their level of attention and be mindful of their thinking and behavioral patterns, especially when stakes are high, fear is blinding, and there is little "space" for genius.

Your Vaganaut

CHAPTER 9.
MAKING SPACE
IN YOUR LIFE

IN THIS BOOK, "making space" is not intended as a mindfulness exercise. It's not about making space for a moment to disconnect and simply be present. Rather, it is about consciously **making space to connect with other people in the moment**. When you consciously make space for a shared moment with others – sustaining full attention on that shared experience – the moment becomes charged with energy.

No matter how small or large, that moment holds the potential to make you feel valued, provide exciting new insights, give you a sense of belonging, fulfill your need to find like-minded people, expand your perspective and knowledge, and/or make you feel you can contribute to others.

But this potential is only unlocked if you can sustain your attention on that shared moment – and particularly when *everyone* can sustain their attention and make space for it by applying the 5 tenets discussed in this book.

You might feel that shared moments can also be painful or intimidating. Those kinds of shared moments happen when people are not consciously joining and are exhibiting behavioral patterns without awareness.

The 5 tenets of making space allow for the moment to provide the best outcomes for everyone by ensuring they join in the moment more consciously. Even if not everyone is making space, if one person does, the outcome is improved. A present person making space for the shared moment has a contagious effect, encouraging others to become more present as well. The more people make space, the harder it becomes for others to not make space for that shared moment.

Building a culture based on the 5 tenets within an organization or community unlocks collective genius and a different level of connection. It is the opposite of sitting at a dinner table together while browsing through your messages; sitting at a meeting table supposedly listening to someone while answering your emails; having a coffee chat while allowing your mind to wander elsewhere; helping your kids with their homework while scrolling through Instagram; sitting in the car with your family while fixating on future worries; arguing at the breakfast table, running the same thinking and behavioral patterns without allowing for the possibility of being wrong; imposing your beliefs and opinions as the only truth on your friends at the bar; running from meeting to meeting not caring about any of them or liking the people; waking up with a cluttered mind, leaving no space to warmly greet loved ones; judging someone sharing their feelings and then seeking distractions to disconnect from the conversation; feeling threatened by anything that undermines your self-perception, allowing no space to observe yourself without clinging to what you identify with.

Your life is a treasure trove of key moments. The most lasting ones are those you've shared. When you deeply connect with people, you're not only addressing your basic human needs for love, belonging, certainty, novelty, growth, and self-realization, but your brain and body also respond neurochemically with oxytocin, dopamine, serotonin, endorphins, and even anandamide, often referred to as the "bliss molecule." A life where you make space for shared moments is a happy life.

Although some claim that social media provides community, it does not replace genuine, "spacious" human connection. It pretends to fulfill our basic human needs but fails to do so, which is why our society is grappling with so much depression. I've noticed that younger generations communicate more on social messaging platforms than by spending time together in real life. A virtual moment of connection can be rewarding, just like a real-life moment, but only if you make space for it, not if you're distracted by gaming or only connecting via short, random messages (and especially if those messages are only emojis and memes). I've also noticed younger generations becoming part of a counter-movement, valuing real connection again over bite-sized, glossed-over content, seeking strategies to manage the distractions that keep them from deeply connecting with friends and family.

We have been wired for social connection through centuries of evolution.

We have been wired for social connection through centuries of evolution. Deep social connection relaxes us, makes us creative, and even keeps us healthy. Loneliness is the number one killer. If you feel you have a hard time connecting, I hope the 5 tenets in this book will help you make space for every shared moment, reprogramming your brain to sustain your attention for deep connection. You can start today to experience every shared moment more consciously by:

- **Working on any resistance to the moment, adopting a mindset that invites it in.**
- **Getting clear on your intentions and who you want to be in this moment.**
- **Finding out how this moment can matter to you, what makes it special or valuable.**
- **Holding space for others to talk, using silence to observe what you want to say before speaking.**
- **Observing your own patterns and those of others, engaging consciously.**

- **Actively listening, taking on different perspectives and opinions, and observing their effect.**
- **Managing your attention by making sense of the conversation for all involved.**
- **Amplifying/appreciating the synergies and nice things arising from the moment.**
- **Being attentive to any outcomes worth acting upon.**
- **Being the first to commit to something that leads to "fruits" from the conversation.**
- **Being the first to activate others, asking for their help or commitment to act together.**

You are switching, finding your hook, depatterning, and anchoring to arrive at a collective inception. This is the key to unlocking collective genius. The more you practice the 5 tenets and make space, the more you'll notice that every shared moment holds a gift, large or small. Your inception will ultimately determine whether that gift is given ample new space in your life.

Every moment you share with others could be a superficial moment of old programs, or you can let go and make space for the moment to reveal its gifts, its secrets. They are always present; you just have to be able to perceive them.

If you live a life of making space for shared moments, you elevate them to co-creation. That simply means allowing synergy to emerge from combining our amazing minds. You aren't stuck in single-minded survival thinking and behavioral patterns, trying to control life, driven by fear and uncertainty. You live accepting things as they are, using that as a foundation, a starting point, for whatever you can co-create with others. All those co-created moments you make space for will leave a mark. Because you elevate them, they will have more emotion, passion, and energy. They will become more prominent memories, shaping you. Making space for shared moments and living them consciously will boost personal growth more than any retreat, book, course, or guru can. It is your birthright to find growth in this life. Every shared moment you make space for provides an invaluable opportunity for growth.

> *Every shared moment you make space for provides an invaluable opportunity for growth.*

As you invest your attention and energy in these shared moments, they become your life, your perspective, shaping who you are. Therefore, your choices of where you spend time and with which kinds of people will determine the life you lead and the person you become. Making space is inviting the world into your life and your very being. Consciously making space for shared moments comes with the responsibility to consciously decide where, with whom, and in what situations you want to grow and fill the treasure chest of your life's key moments.

Those key moments make up your life and who you are, and they influence who you will become, not your desired destinations in the future. It is clichéd, but the journey is truly more important than the destination. If you allow a lot of unhappiness in your life just to achieve a soupcon of an ideal or wealthy future, you will build a life of unhappy moments, shaping who you are. When you arrive at your desired destination, if ever you do, the life that led you there will have shaped you so much that you probably won't even be able to enjoy it. If you see life as a grand unraveling adventure where every moment you make space for holds a gift, which you can decide deserves (or doesn't) even more space in your life, you will be living in the moment.

The 5 tenets of making space are simple. They are common sense. The idea that every shared moment has the potential for co-creation, with yourself as the only obstacle, is an intuitive truth. The concept of collective genius, a bond of abilities, a thriving community, and being an integral part of something amazing – the beauty of serendipity, synergy, and synchronicity – is something we unconsciously seek in all we do. But it can feel unattainable. With the horrible things humans can do to each other, you might have lost confidence and lost touch with your inner child, who only wanted to make space for the world to reveal itself. Because we are social beings, connecting is in our nature. Even if it lies underneath layers of disappointment, pain, and frustrations. It just takes a little attention, your most valuable asset. It only needs you to direct your attention a bit differently and more consciously. It only takes investing your energy a little more intentionally. And you will soon witness the beauty of collective intelligence and the enormous potential we have together in our shared moments.

Your attention creates your reality. Use it wisely.

Dear Diary,

I know. It has been a while. But I feel that the goal of writing to you has been attained. I felt a bit empty before we met. I was envious of other people's life portrayed so beautifully on their socials. I didn't feel appreciated at work and felt mistreated with every acknowledgment and promotion that went to someone else. I had a hard time chasing my dreams, even understanding what my dreams were. What did I want out of life? Writing to you was the best thing I could ever do. I was looking to grow out of the mindset I had. I am happy to tell you that I have now managed to kickstart a culture of "making space" at work. For me, this is the pinnacle of my journey in space. It didn't happen by imposing frameworks, rules, or any other "clutter." It scaled because I helped my colleagues find their own "hook" for making more space. And boy, did they find their hooks. I didn't even have to create language for certain principles; they created their own. They started sharing their approaches and experiences with each other without any internal campaigns. It even spread naturally across all management layers. Our leaders now prioritize holding space above expressing their leading opinions. So many colleagues have also shared their personal stories about how this influenced their friendships, relationships, predicaments with family members, and understanding of what makes them happy, all because they are making space whenever they can. I have witnessed our collective genius on multiple occasions, very consciously, and it is beautiful. When people have a clear intention about who they want to be for others, when they find their groove in the moment, when they don't believe their own thoughts so much, when they prioritize the shared moment above all distractions in life, honoring it, and when they find meaning in contributing with others, incredible outcomes are brought to life. This journey opened a new chapter in my life. I stopped chasing future happiness and found all the joy I needed in exploring the potential of collective genius, investing my full attention in everyday shared moments.

Your Vaganaut

AFTERWORD
By Alwin Put & Julie Harris

AP: When I was writing *Captains of Leadership: Build Your Facilitative Confidence*, I already felt I wanted to write a second book about "making space" for co-creation. In the last years, after publishing *Captains*, as I witnessed the struggle people face with managing their attention for great co-creation, I knew it was time to start writing again. Opposite to writing *Captains*, I wasn't very clear about how to structure the content, but I was highly motivated to bring the message out there. When I tried to outline the content of the book by writing an article on "making space," some concepts took more shape, but it was far from a coherent vision. That made it a bit of a scary start, not being able to envision the end result. I covered a lot of ground, literally, walking hours through nature just to get my thoughts straight while writing the book. It was very important to me that I would be sharing wisdom, not knowledge. I wanted to write about my practices when making space in a storytelling way so everyone can easily relate and feel the urge to start experimenting with space. Some explanations about the tenets felt like stating the obvious, and some felt overcomplicated, turning a two-step process into a ten-part saga. Unexpectedly, it was quite a challenge to write about such an intuitive practice as "making space" in a way that makes it very accessible to everyone and encourages them to experiment.

JH: I remember reading the proofs of *Captains of Leadership* and thinking, "Wow! There is so much here." So much of the unspoken. I also felt it was a book I would use as a guide, one I would dip back into every time I designed and delivered a workshop. And you know what? That's what it turned out to be. A reference manual, an *aide memoire*, as we say in French, that has accompanied me to Los Angeles, London, and Paris for each and every workshop I design and deliver. It lives in my carry-on and is a volume I pull out on planes, in hotel rooms, and shhhhh … don't tell anyone … in powder rooms (during workshop breaks). More recently, Alwin's article on Making Space came across my desk. I had another "There is so much here" moment. Even though it was in its nascent stages, I could discern a strong structure and potential within its pages. As it developed, story by story, like honey drizzled into plain yogurt, the read sweetened.

AP: I don't think there is anything more satisfying for an author than being told his book is frequently used as a guide. *Captains* was specifically written for facilitators, people who build and lead workshops at work. As a facilitator myself, I found writing the book to be like sharing my notes with my peers. *Unlock Collective Genius* is different. It required me to reflect deeply on my personal life. Writing this book pushed me to make sense of the things I do to make space. Making space has always been an integral part of my life, as I am a serial daydreamer struggling with focus issues from an early age. I have always had problems doing focused work from morning to evening. I needed to learn how to manage my attention, and it eventually became second nature. Having struggled with managing my own attention, I recognize very quickly if someone's attention is "elsewhere." I have noticed that this has become a huge obstacle to creativity and co-creation in the last few years. My intention is more than ever to write a *personal guide to making space* that anyone can apply at work and in their private lives. I hope my personal practices and the way they are broken down into building blocks can kickstart a movement of making space. A counter-movement against allowing your mind to become programmed for distractions, blocking your creativity and co-creative genius. I wonder if the 5 tenets are a strong enough antidote in all situations.

JH: This makes me smile. It always does – Alwin, when he is thinking "out loud." He writes just like he thinks. Did you see how he moved from sharing notes on his facilitator experience and wisdom in *Captains* to his personal story to his personal challenges to his desire to share his learning with the world – and then to his own quiet doubt: are the 5 tenets strong enough for all situations? He often does macro to micro and back to macro. I love it. But to his question, of course, the 5 tenets aren't the foolproof antidote! There is no magic formula for every single situation or context. Good heavens, no! And if we had such a formula, there'd be no further room for growth. If you've ever been a parent, you'll get this. **Just when you think you've figured it out** (your little one just fell asleep on time and without tears – or they've just gone off to university and they're making new friends), **everything gets switched up** (your little one does NOT fall asleep the following week with the same technique – or your college student calls homesick and your soothing words aren't doing a darned thing to help). My hope is that this book is a doorstopper in the best possible way. I can see it holding the door open to let fresh air in, new people in and out, and space for even more growth. This book isn't an end. It's the means.

AP: Luckily, your magical wordsmithing can find the red thread in all the macro-ing and micro-ing throughout this book, Julie, leading us to the ideal label for the book. A doorstopper that keeps the door open to our inner world. This book has established its purpose if it helps you, dear reader, spend time with people more consciously and deliberately. And while doing so, learning a great deal more about yourself. The 5 tenets, indeed, are not foolproof; nor are they shiny, magic bullets. They are an invitation to manage your attention with intent. If we allow a whirlwind of information to take us everywhere and nowhere every day, the only possible result is a distracted mind with little self-love. We are all the same, and we are completely different. The 5 tenets are a proposition to invest and sustain your attention more deeply in the moments you share with others, as our encounters are the birthplace of creation and lessons in humanity. We often fail to prioritize shared moments with others, allowing distractions to take precedence. However, these moments have the potential to *Unlock Collective Genius* providing us with purpose, connection, growth, and significance. By making space for and with others, we take ownership of our co-creative powers.

Lower your resistance. Find your groove. Let go to see things differently. Keep charging that moment until you have crystallized the shared desired outcome. There really is no limit to unlocking collective genius – besides your willingness to make space for it.

Your Vaganauts

GLOSSARY

I extend my deepest appreciation to you. I am honored that you were willing to sustain your attention to finish this book, making space for it and allowing it to become part of your life. In my style of writing, I often use terms in unconventional ways, which may require additional explanation. Some of these terms can also serve as ideal phrases to shape a language for "making space" – terms that will allow you to easily reference experiences and concepts when discussing "making space" with your friends, family, and colleagues. Allow me to provide you with some extra context and explanation for these terms.

Typically, a glossary of terms is alphabetized. We have decided to list the terms in order of use in the book. This way it also serves as a brief summary.

Moment
A moment is an experience that takes up a chunk of your time and a chunk of your attention. It has a beginning and an end and consists of a situation. When the situation involves other people, it is considered a shared moment. Every shared moment is an encounter between different minds and different perspectives. Such encounters always have the potential to enrich new insights and for synergy. Our life consists of all these moments. If we can elevate some of them, we are increasing our quality of life.

(Deep) Space
Space is the result of your level of attention to a moment. This could be a shared moment. A higher level of sustained attention to a shared moment results in deeper space for deeper connection. When your attention is not distracted by things outside the moment that are irrelevant to the situation or by thoughts that keep you from connecting with others who are sharing the moment, you have made space for co-creation. You have made space for the unknown to arise, for novelty and ingenuity.

Vaganaut
"Vaga-" is derived from "Vagal Nerve," which is the longest cranial nerve in the human body. This nerve plays a crucial role in helping your body relax and calm down by counteracting stress responses. Additionally, the vagal nerve influences mood, immune function, and communication between the gut and brain. It promotes feelings of connection and trust with others, supporting social relationships and emotional well-being. The suffix "–naut" is a reference to someone who explores or travels in a specific context. It is derived from the Greek word "nautes," meaning sailor or navigator, implying someone who navigates or journeys within a particular domain or field. "Vaganaut" is a combination of both "Vaga-" and "-naut" to refer to an individual who enjoys making and exploring space to unlock the potential of a shared moment.

Collaboration
Collaboration in this book is used to refer to that moment when you actively spend time together working on a specific topic. Working in this context does not necessarily mean you are coming up with new interpretations and deepening your understanding. It refers to merely exchanging information to get things done.

Co-creation
The moment when individuals come together to create something new, leveraging each other's unique perspectives and expertise. The key difference between co-creation and collaboration lies in the fact that the people involved in co-creation work together to produce a result that is greater than the sum of their individual contributions. This synergistic approach leads to a higher level of interpretation and innovation rather than merely settling for compromises.

Tenet
This book intentionally makes use of the word "tenet" instead of "principles" because "making space" is an ideology. The benefits of "making space" are fundamental beliefs for a culture of creativity and connection. The 5 tenets characterize the philosophy of experiencing shared moments more consciously to unlock collective potential, the genius. A tenet is a belief that nurtures a mindset.

Design Thinking
A human-centered approach to problem-solving that emphasizes empathy, creativity, and iterative prototyping to develop innovative solutions that meet user needs effectively and sustainably. This book refers to Design Thinking as a perfect example of co-creation that requires deep space to be successful.

Switch
Switching is the capability of directing your attention and shaping your intention from one moment to another. It involves working through any resistance for the moment to happen and becoming very conscious about your personal intentions for the moment.

A Firm "Yes"
When you decide to be completely part of a moment with your full attention, having no resistance whatsoever to investing your time and energy.

Hook
Your personal reason why you want to invest all your attention in the moment. Why the moment matters to you. It is what keeps you hooked into the moment.

Layered Hook
A hook can be a practical or superficial reason to keep your attention in the moment. A reason that has little emotional load. It could also be a profound reason that touches on your personal values in life or the way you want or don't want to be perceived by other people. In that sense, the hook in this book is presented as layered with superficial top layers and more emotionally loaded mid- and deep layers. The deeper the layer, the closer it gets to your basic needs in life.

Hook Triangle
The hook is explained as a triangle consisting of three important angles: the aspect that catches your attention, how important it is to your idea of self, and how it impacts the way others see you. In short, the trigger, self, and context. The triangle is a simple and powerful way to explain that something that moves you will always have some kind of opportunity to trigger you; it will resonate with your beliefs and values, and it influences your social equity or "position."

Trigger
A trigger within the context of a hook is the aspect of the moment that grabs your attention. Usually, it is a chance, an opportunity, something that makes it worthwhile to have the moment. At first, you don't necessarily understand why it triggers you. Therefore, there is a triangular approach to figuring out what it means to you personally and how it impacts your relationship with others.

Harmonize Hooks
A hook triangle has different layers of interpretation, with the top layers being more superficial and less emotionally charged. Deep layers touch upon sensitive topics and, therefore, trigger more emotions. Harmonizing the hook involves finding the optimal layer that provides the most motivation. If you dig too deep, you might uncover pains and frustrations that have a paralyzing rather than motivational effect. Conversely, if you remain too shallow, the hook may not be strong enough to compete with other attention grabbers during the shared moment. The key is to find the sweet spot – the layer that resonates most strongly with the reasons why you want to keep your full attention on this shared moment.

Patterns
Repeated thinking and behavior that happen unconsciously in a habitual way. Patterns are a result of programming the way you respond to certain situations. Programming is your brain organizing neural connections based on experiences and interactions with your environment.

Depatterning
The act of recognizing and breaking your habitual patterns to arrive at new insights, new solutions, and new interpretations. Patterns repeat the known; depatterning makes space for the unknown.

Genius in the Bottle
When you repeat your typical thinking and behavior without being conscious of it, you are in the bottle. When you identify with your beliefs, when you believe your every thought, when you only see one truth, you are in the bottle. In the bottle, you can't see the label. In the bottle, you can't observe yourself to stop identifying with your thinking. A genius is characterized by profound insight and exceptional originality. That genius is in every one of us, but it can get stuck in the bottle. Our genius, and our collective genius, comes out of the bottle if we come out of the bottle. By letting go of rigid thinking and making space for the unknown, our genius comes out of the bottle.

Vagus Nerve
The vagus nerve (also called the vagal nerve), or tenth cranial nerve (CN X), is a critical component of the autonomic nervous system responsible for regulating involuntary bodily functions, such as heart rate, digestion, and respiratory rate. It is the longest cranial nerve, extending from the brainstem to multiple organs in the chest and abdomen. Additionally, the vagus nerve plays a significant role in promoting social interaction and emotional bonding by influencing facial expressions, vocalization, and emotional responses, contributing to feelings of safety, trust, and connection in social settings.

Synchronize States
Synchronizing states in this book refers to a group activity that aligns the respiratory and heart rates among participants to induce a collective, relaxed state. This activity involves collective breathing exercises. By synchronizing states, people become more open to each other and thus ready for co-creation.

Depatterning Tactics
Tactics that can be applied in workshops to help participants shift their perspective and see things differently with the goal of arriving at better interpretations and conclusions. This may involve tasking participants with preparing an extreme point of view and confronting opposite extreme perspectives. This approach helps to broaden their understanding of the situation by

exposing them to a wide range of viewpoints. These tactics are designed to stir up controversy and ensure that everything is brought out into the open, covering all blind spots during the co-creation process.

Anchoring
Anchoring sustains your attention when making space for a moment to come into existence. Anchors serve as attention grabbers within the moment, helping to compete against other potential distractions outside of the moment. Everyone's attention weakens after a while. Anchoring brings your attention back whenever it drifts off.

M.O.R.E.
This is an acronym that refers to the four different ways to anchor your attention to the moment. The **M** stands for **M**oment, implying you anchor your attention by acknowledging the beauty of the moment. The **O** stands for **O**rganize, implying you anchor your attention by recapping the progress made. The **R** stands for **R**eason, implying you anchor your attention by reminding yourself of your hook. The **E** stands for **E**xplore, implying you anchor your attention by being interested in whatever comes out of the synergy of the moment. M.O.R.E., in itself as a word, expresses the desire to have "more" of the moment by reinvesting your attention in it again and again.

Inception
The seed planted by the co-creation that can grow into the outcomes when you act upon it. It is the ultimate anchor that keeps your attention invested in bringing the outcomes to life. It is your strategy to manifest. Your strategy to keep yourself motivated, ensuring the necessary ability and ongoing prompting to make it happen.

The Ultimate Anchor
The ultimate anchor, inception, is set to be the strongest anchoring during a shared moment. It is about making space to make space for action in the future. It is also called inception, as it should provide a drive so strong that it overcomes all the obstacles in your way. The ultimate anchor that creates grit, perseverance, and a sense of ownership.

Ownership
The feeling of responsibility to see things through until they are completed. In large organizations with numerous stakeholders and potential conflicts, nurturing a sense of ownership among individuals can be one of the biggest challenges. People may become confused about what is expected of them and may be reluctant to take on significant responsibility, particularly in a hostile environment. Ownership is the direct result of strong inception.

Hook Twist
The hook is the answer to the question, "In what way can this matter to me?" It refers to the most compelling reason someone should continue investing their attention in the moment. It is a passive way of finding meaning. On the other hand, the hook twist answers the question, "In what way can I matter to achieving this outcome?" It refers to what you can actively contribute when bringing a desired outcome to life. This twist is an active form of self-actualization, where you utilize your expertise, talent, and capabilities to contribute to common goals. Together, the hook and hook twist serve as powerful motivators to nurture ownership.

Circular Conversations
When the same arguments are repeated by the same or different people in similar or different words. The conversation does not really progress, although attention and energy are invested. It goes around and around without producing any new significant insights.

Meeting Culture
The collective behavior and habits related to setting up, leading, participating, and acting upon the outcomes of meetings or gatherings within organizations. These habits can include inviting people without providing them with a clear personal reason to join, inviting as many people as possible to gain buy-in, scheduling meetings simply to scratch topics off a to-do list, having marathons of half-hour meetings throughout the day, or conducting long-winded meetings dominated by a few vocal individuals. Other aspects of meeting culture may include holding meetings without actionable minutes, relying predominantly on online meetings, keeping cameras off, arriving late and leaving early, keeping laptops open during meetings, and lacking ownership at the end of meetings. Additionally, meeting culture can be characterized by a lack of structured conversations during meetings.

Culture of "Making Space"
The collective behavior related to applying the 5 tenets of making space at any shared moment with the aim of deeper connections and better outcomes.

Collective Genius
The synergistic power of a group to co-create and achieve extraordinary results, making space to leverage diverse perspectives and skills. By tapping into collective intelligence and creativity, a team can make significant strides beyond what the individuals can accomplish alone.

ACKNOWLEDGMENTS

This is my second book. It exists only because of the love and support I receive from some very special people in my life. I am blessed and privileged to be able to enjoy the deep connection I have with them.

ANNELIES – The fire just keeps burning, and it fuels my creativity and drive to create. You remain my moral compass, my beacon, and my most sincere critic. Your common sense has a grounding effect on me. This second book also exists because of your love and support.

MAGNUS – Your wit and enthusiasm give me energy every day. I am in awe, watching you handle growing up in this frantic world, which is completely different from the world I grew up in. You have inspired so many stories and concepts in this book. It is a privilege to be your father!

SVANTE – I love the way your mind works, the things you notice, the genius in your interpretations of the world. It inspires me to look at this world from different perspectives. Already at your young age, you dazzle me with your strong character. It is a privilege to be your father!

IDA VANDEPOEL – In your late 70s, you are still full of youthfulness and *joie de vivre*. You are the source of my optimism and altruism. The drive to bring a message to the world the best way I can to help people make sense of creativity and co-creation stems from your loving parenting. Thank you for being such a great mom.

JOS PUT – Dad, I miss you. I miss our conversations. I wish you could have read this one as well. I am so curious about your take on it. You are in my mind whenever I write.

JULIE HARRIS – Your incredible writing skills, your intellectual support, and your vast experience in facilitation and coaching have been essential to creating this book. This wouldn't have been possible without having the perfect ally. Thank you so much!

KEVIN HAESEN – Your wisdom and friendship have inspired my writing tremendously. Our conversations always bring so much clarity to life's difficulties and mysteries. You are one of the most heart-centered people I know. The world needs more Kevins.

OLIVIER HENS - A Captain of Leadership, a true ambassador of facilitation, a great friend to have, and a fantastic soundboard to keep things down to earth. The way you can say things exactly, to the point, with no fuzz and no sugar coating, has helped me to keep it real and practical.

EVA BRUCHEZ - Even though we only have the chance to talk now and then, the conversations are always mind-blowing. Whenever I want to write something or develop a new concept, I know I need to run it by you first to sharpen my perspective on it. Thank you for being such a great supporter of my work.

TINE VAN WEL - You have done it again, Tine! Because of your skills, both books look amazing. Your graphic design uplifts the reading experience and creates a signature look and feel to the series. Your work is top-notch!

HARM VAN KESSEL (AND EVERYONE AT BIS PUBLISHERS) - Thank you so much for the opportunity to get my stories out there. It is an honor to write for BIS Publishers.

And to all the amazing Captains I have gotten to know well over the years … Guy de Cock, Christophe Zurn, Felipe Camara, Stephan Croix, Colette Forma, Samuel Van Braekel, Marc Bolick, Mike Mannix, Clemens Froelich, Arne Van Oosterom … and all the wonderful people I met in my training programs and workshops, thank you so much for inspiring me. This book was written in honor of all of you.